LEADERSHIP
ISN'T FOR
COWARDS

LEADERSHIP
ISN'T FOR
COWARDS

How to DRIVE PERFORMANCE
by CHALLENGING PEOPLE
and CONFRONTING PROBLEMS

MIKE STAVER

WILEY

John Wiley & Sons, Inc.

Published by John Wiley & Sons, Inc., Hoboken, New Jersey.
Published simultaneously in Canada.

For general information on our other products and services or for technical support, please contact our Customer Care Department within the United States at (800) 762-2974, outside the United States at (317) 572-3993 or fax (317) 572-4002.

Wiley publishes in a variety of print and electronic formats and by print-on-demand. Some material included with standard print versions of this book may not be included in e-books or in print-on-demand. If this book refers to media such as a CD or DVD that is not included in the version you purchased, you may download this material at http://booksupport.wiley.com. For more information about Wiley products, visit www.wiley.com.

ISBN 978-1-118-17683-2 (cloth); ISBN 978-1-118-22713-8 (ebk);
ISBN 978-1-118-24023-6 (ebk); ISBN 978-1-118-26484-3 (ebk)

Printed in the United States of America
10 9 8 7 6 5 4 3 2 1

CONTENTS

ACKNOWLEDGMENTS

Years ago I wrote the keynote "Leadership Isn't for Cowards." Thousands of people have heard it in various versions. To all of you, thank you for unknowingly helping me create this book. Your participation in those keynotes helped me form my thoughts and solidify what I believe it means to live and lead with courage.

My deepest thanks to my coaching clients who prove every day that leading courageously really is the best way to lead. In particular I am thankful to the members of StaverConnect. Your leadership and willingness to share openly and honestly with each other is an outstanding example of courageous leadership.

To the team at The Staver Group, Bobbie Stanton, Mary Anne Rybak, Sondra Ulin, and Maxx McInerney, thank you for keeping our customers happy, things running smoothly, and me sane. I am grateful for your unique and important contributions to the lives of the leaders we serve.

Deborah Schindlar, Peter Knox, Tiffany Colon, and everyone at John Wiley & Sons, thank you for all you have done to make this project successful. You have each been supportive and smart, and that is a great combination! A special thanks to Dan Ambrosio, editor at Wiley, from our initial conversation right through the entire project you have had a perfect blend of enthusiasm and guidance. Thank you for this opportunity.

Amy Claire, not only are you an amazing artist of the English language but you are also the perfect blend of insight, critique, and support. Your understanding of my style and voice combined with your editorial skill gave me great peace of mind and confidence! Thank you. I am forever grateful to Michael for introducing us.

Finally to all of my friends and family who have encouraged, and believed in me and this work! I noticed and I appreciate you very much!

YOU ARE MESSING WITH PEOPLE'S LIVES

This section lays the foundation for all that follows in the rest of the book. You will be challenged to understand the depth and breadth of leadership and to see how doing so can transform the way you lead. You will receive a clearer understanding of organizational culture and realize the true extent of your own impact. The journey begins here.

CHAPTER 1

Do You Know What You Are Doing?

For your sake, let's hope you answered that question with a resounding "sometimes." I hope you are like the rest of us, having to stop on some days and wonder what you were thinking when you said yes to leadership. The fact is, most leaders have times in their lives when they find themselves asking, "Do I know what I'm doing?" It's a normal and expected part of being in a role where you influence people.

You first have to know and accept one major thing that you are doing as a leader . . .

You are messing with people's lives!

(I'm not sure how much more clearly I can say that.)

> You are messing with people's lives!

The day you said yes to someone, somewhere up in your organization, and decided to join the ranks of leaders, you decided (with complete false confidence) that you had the willingness and ability to tell other people what to do.

Or maybe you didn't. Maybe you were recruited—placed in a leadership class and given three points and a poem on how to lead before you were tossed the keys and wished good luck.

Maybe you entered into a management training program with wide-eyed enthusiasm and a commitment to change the world.

Maybe you decided that you would take a stab at starting your own business. Spreading your entrepreneurial wings, you jumped into the world of business ownership with all of its thrills and risks.

Whatever the case, your decision to say yes to leadership was driven by something—a need to help others, to make more money, to save the world, to boost your self-esteem, to make a difference, or some other reason. Regardless of your reason, your choice resulted in one simple fact: You began *messing with people's lives*. You may not have realized it or wanted it, but that's what happened.

Unfortunately, most leaders do not start with that knowledge. They don't start with a clear and compelling understanding of the real challenges facing them. Their understanding is diluted with operational plans, goal setting, revenue and sales forecasts, cash flow, HR compliance, and the magical bottom line. While all of those are important, they're not the *most* important. How you influence others is the most important.

It takes courage to accept the challenge of influencing another person. Do not underestimate that challenge. In most cases, the people who report directly to you will spend more time with you than with their families. You will occupy their thoughts (positively or negatively) more than most other people, and you will be the subject of stories around the bar or the dinner table more times than you can imagine. When they go to lunch they will talk about you. When you lead meetings they will evaluate you. You are on their minds, whether you want to be or not. Leadership is not a job for cowards!

It's time to adjust your perspective on your job as a leader. You do not lead an organization, department, or group, and your people do not follow strategic plans, fancy goals, or year-end reports. They follow a person. If you are their leader, that person needs to be you. Begin with the idea of influence and your role will start to take shape.

I sat in a room with ten high-level executives from the same industry. I had been invited to speak to them about courage. It was a train wreck. After the train wreck there was dinner and a reception. At the reception, I was talking with the senior vice president of a large company. Once he loosened up a little and realized I wasn't there to coach him or diagnose him, he shared an interesting story.

He had been a top salesperson in his company for years. He was relentless in his pursuit of the numbers and the prestige that comes with being a top performer. He always exceeded expectations and thought he was more or less guaranteed the highest and best awards the company had. He was promoted to sales manager and, true to form, his team hit it out of the park every quarter. He was clearly a star and wasn't afraid to throw his success and influence around to get what he wanted.

One day his boss called him into his office and told him that if things didn't change, he would be fired. He almost fell off the chair. "Me? The superhero? The guy who led the most successful team in the company? How could this be?"

Then his boss hit him right between the eyes. He told him that his team hated him, the other teams disrespected him, and he didn't have a clue about how to relate to people. People were just a means to an end for him. The next thing he knew, they had hired a coach for him and he began *the* most difficult transformation of his career. Without the intervention of his insightful boss, it is likely his career would have been derailed. With all of the prizes and plaques and accolades, he still would have failed.

Now before you go off saying, "Oh, I'm nothing like that," just take a step back and look at the real moral of that story. Don't compare your behavior to his; compare your awareness. His trouble was as much about his awareness as it was his actual behavior. Even though he was wildly successful, he didn't know what he was doing. Oh, he had the technical expertise, but he didn't have any insight into the extent to which he was messing with people's lives. He didn't understand that his award-winning results had a great price. He made money but lost the respect of those he worked with and, worse, he damaged the relationships that were necessary to his success. He was blinded by his great results and lack of awareness.

In his case, he was lucky enough to have a boss who stopped him in his tracks and plainly said, "Hey, not only are you messing *with* people's lives, but you are also messing *up* people's lives." What's fortunate is that his boss was courageous enough to tell him, in so many words, that all his success was not worth it to the company unless he made some major changes. His boss understood how to be influential in a constructive way. He possessed and demonstrated an understanding of his influence.

Do you know what you are doing? Do you have the courage to honestly answer that question? Here are five questions to get you started:

1. Take an honest look at your leadership mindset. Do you appreciate and respect the fact that you are messing with people's lives? What makes you think that?

2. Is that awareness apparent in the way you carry yourself and interact with the people you influence? Take a moment to write down or think about a few times when you have successfully used your influence.

3. Do you have balance between the results you create and the human impact of those results? Have there been times when the cost to your relationships was too high, even though the results were good? What would you do differently in the future?

4. Find a person you trust to give you the clear and constructive truth about the positive and negative impact of your behavior. What did they say?

5. What are some small, incremental adjustments you can make to your behavior to emphasize the positive impacts?

For a download of a worksheet for this chapter and others please go to www.leadershipisntforcowards.com or scan the QR code.

Leadership Isn't for
Cowards Workbook

CHAPTER 2

How Much of an Impact Are You Really Having?

Don't worry for a second about whether or not you are having an impact. You are. The question is whether the impact you are having is the impact that will make you proud years from now. Are you satisfied that you hit the numbers and brought home the profit, or do your values demand that you have greater and more profound impact on your workplace and on the people you influence?

Consider this on a variety of levels: What impact are you having on the values of your people? Do you model the kind of character that would make you a compelling figure to follow? What impact are you having on your direct reports' emotional states? Are they happy to work for you? Do they feel good about their work? Are they fairly compensated? Do you encourage personal development? To what extent do your followers feel better about who they are because of the way you lead?

If your direct reports are going to talk about you behind your back (and they are) then you had better get busy influencing that gossip. Right now, as you read this sentence, someone who reports to you is out there telling a story about you. That story is about the impact you have on them. While they may tell stories about some cool thing you did or some deal you closed or some speech you gave, your real power comes from how you affect them as individuals. That is what they will talk about the most, and that is what they will remember about you.

Courageous leadership involves developing clarity and awareness about the impact you want to have on those you lead. There is risk involved in being more personal and more engaged with your

> Courageous leadership involves developing clarity and awareness about the impact you want to have on those that you lead.

followers. It takes courage to reveal your core values and admit your weaknesses to your team. It takes courage to raise your voice and say, "Follow me!" It takes courage to ask people to trust you with the uncertainty of the next quarter's business plan. You have to earn that trust. If you get in front of them and ask them to follow you, you'd better be clear about where you are headed and why they should go there. You'd better be certain that they are each personally and powerfully connected to you and the future you see.

On a recent teleconference, I asked a company's vice president about the current mindset of the followers in his part of the organization. I found his response both refreshingly authentic and extremely troubling all at once. He said, "They're skeptical about the future of our company. They trust the leaders they report to but lack confidence in those higher up in the organization. They feel disconnected from the bigger picture. They aren't sure that the C-level executives really understand what they are dealing with every day."

In other words, the followers didn't have confidence that the senior leaders knew what they were doing. Uncertainty and skepticism spread throughout the organization because of the leaders' lack of clarity about where the company was headed and how that would affect everyone.

So how do you take control of your impact?

There are two elements in your leadership impact: scientific and artistic. The scientific side encompasses everything a leader has to do every day to execute the fundamental processes of the business: making widgets, getting widgets into stores, writing reports about widgets, making the widget makers happy, evaluating the competitive widget producers in the market . . . you get the idea.

The artistic side is all about answering personal questions: *What are my values? How do I communicate them to the culture? How do I connect those I lead to what I believe? How do I create the right kind of culture for the people who follow me? What type of experiences do I need to create for my followers so that they have the greatest chance for success? Are they really following me, or are they simply complying with directives?* (Those aren't rhetorical questions. Answer them! Evaluate how your leadership behaviors measure up to your answers.)

Your followers care less about the scientific side of your leadership and more about the artistic side. Have you ever known a leader who was technically competent but was asked to leave the company because his or her artistic leadership was so pathetic? Someone who could meet the numbers but made everyone miserable in the process? Of course you do. You've probably worked for someone like that, and you probably hated every minute of it. Don't let that happen to your own leadership.

Most leaders focus almost exclusively on the scientific aspects of leadership throughout their careers. I am not suggesting that there is anything wrong with the scientific side. I *am* suggesting that the best leaders find a balance. They are able to meet their numbers and understand the stress their people experience. They are able to create a positive customer experience and develop a great place to work. They are able to demand excellence and hold true to their core values.

For many, the artistic side makes them uncomfortable. They can get their heads around numbers. They can measure and quantify cash flow, balance sheets, and profit and loss statements. They see values and culture as intimidating, unquantifiable things. There are those who go so far as to act like the artistic side of leadership doesn't produce tangible results. Nothing could be further from the truth!

It takes courage to investigate the pieces of the business that you can't neatly and cleanly pin down. It takes courage to look inward and get clarity on what you believe. Once you have clarity, it takes courage to step up and talk about how those beliefs have impact on the work you and your followers do. It requires introspection, emotional intelligence, and a sense of focus that is different from what most of us were taught in business school. You are lost in the woods if you think you can have positive and productive impact while ignoring the artistic side of your leadership. In the next chapter, we'll discuss the courage you need to do this,

> You are lost in the woods if you think you can have positive and productive impact while ignoring the artistic side of your leadership.

but for now, the following three steps will help you start to emphasize the artistic side of your leadership and get control of your impact.

1. Evaluate where you spend the majority of your energy. Are you more comfortable in the scientific elements of your leadership or the artistic ones? (I know you think you are balanced, but all of us favor one over the other, if only slightly.)

2. Clarify the impact you are having on those you lead. Use a 360 assessment, a focus group, or hypnosis (just kidding). Find out what your subordinates think about your impact.

3. Write down specific steps to help you balance your impact and make it more intentional.

For a download of a worksheet for this chapter and others please go to www.leadershipisntforcowards.com or scan the QR code.

Leadership Isn't for
Cowards Workbook

CHAPTER 3

Are You a Coward?

Relax! I'm not calling you a coward . . . yet. I am simply asking you to take a moment to evaluate the extent to which courage and fear influence the way you live and work. I am not here to judge—just to ask tough questions. What are you afraid of? What is the most courageous thing you have done or decision you have made in the last 12 months? What is a courageous decision you need to make but haven't? How much are you willing to lose to do the right thing? I will leave the judging in your capable hands.

What comes to mind when you hear the word *courage?*

A firefighter rushing into a burning building. Steve Jobs first releasing the iPod. Aron Ralston cutting off his arm to free himself from a boulder. Any of the ordinary men and women who raise children, stand up for unpopular beliefs, sit by the bedsides of dying loved ones, or quietly carry on in the face of hardship and tragedy.

The *American Heritage Dictionary* defines courage as "the state or quality of mind or spirit that enables one to face danger, fear, or vicissitudes with self-possession, confidence, and resolution; bravery."[1]

Some say you either have it or you don't. I suppose that's true for a single moment in time, but overall, courage can, and should, be developed.

Courage, for the purposes of this book, has to do with the willingness to face what needs to be faced and to do what needs to be done. It involves making your leadership heartbeat felt by those around you. To do this, you must stand by your values in every aspect

---

[1] "Courage," *American Heritage Dictionary*, 5th ed. (2011). http://ahdictionary.com.

> Courage, for the purposes of this book, has to do with the willingness to face what needs to be faced and to do what needs to be done.

of your life, whether it's in business, the community where you live, or your interactions with the people you influence. It is a relentless commitment to achieving results, with an unyielding focus on your values. It is the boldness necessary to challenge people and confront problems head-on. In short, courage is a way of life.

With that in mind, I want you to answer some of the toughest questions you will ever consider:

- What do you believe?
- What are your core values?
- To what extent are you living and leading in alignment with those beliefs and values?
- Most importantly, why should people follow you? Why should they subject themselves to your leadership for eight or more hours a day? (Don't say, "Because I'm the boss.")

So how do you figure out what you value, and how do you communicate that to others? It's really not complicated. Show me what you do, and I will show you what you value. What you say you value doesn't matter; your behavior reflects what you *actually* value. The question is, are you modeling the values you want to model? Have you taken the time to sit down and think about what your values are and write them down? Make them a living, breathing part of your leadership. They are what should be driving every decision. Your core values are the most compelling reason for a person to follow you. You must be clear about what they are and they must be talked about and lived in every area of your leadership. Do not underestimate their impact and the ability they have to create results that will be the envy of many.

Occasionally people say to me, "That's not true, Mike. You're a little harsh! Can't people value something, even though they don't act on it?"

Well yes, I am a little harsh. Therefore, may I harshly and respectfully say, "No. That can't happen." What you do is the direct result of what you value *most*. You may think you value other things, but they're not as important to you as the things you actually do.

You figured out what you want your values to be (at least, you did if you followed the instructions). So now, either adjust what you say your values are, or adjust your behavior to align with your stated values. Close the gap between what you say you want to accomplish and what you are willing to do to accomplish it.

The two primary values I want to challenge you to adopt are authenticity and personal responsibility. They will bring you the greatest sense of courage you have ever experienced. They will drive your personal and professional performance to higher levels. And yet, few leaders fully adopt them. In my coaching practice, I am always amazed at how many excuses and how much time is wasted by leaders displacing responsibility. If you are going to lead, then perhaps learning to be authentic and accept responsibility is the most courageous place to start.

> If you are going to lead, then perhaps learning to be authentic and accept responsibility is the most courageous place to start.

I know, I know, it's hard and challenging, but the bottom line is: Leadership isn't for cowards. This is where your courage comes in. If you are going to mess with people's lives (and you are), you'd better align your behaviors with your talk. If you don't, they will sniff you out and bust your credibility to pieces. You could lose the respect of your followers, the credibility you have worked to build with your customers, and, worst of all, you could ultimately lose your job. It's serious.

Here's the scary part: in most cases, you will never know. Your followers will never tell you about their loss of respect, unless someone like me comes along and suggests an office evaluation. Then, once they say what they really think of you—*bam!*— you will say, "Oh my gosh. I had no idea. I didn't know my behavior would have that effect." Now you do.

I am reminded of the leader of a mid-sized company who preached the value of integrity every day but allowed his number-one salesperson to run roughshod over everyone in the organization, pirating leads meant for other workers, in order to meet the numbers. He sacrificed the artistic side of his leadership for the scientific. Ultimately, he was forced to fire the salesperson and struggled to regain the respect of the rest of the sales team. The financial benefits were quickly lost in the unintended consequences of failing to address the damaging results. Selling out to the balance sheet like this will usually have short-term gains, but the long-term results of such short-sightedness leave many organizations on the scrap heap, both literally and morally.

It takes courage to confront high-performing employees who aren't in alignment with the way you want the culture to operate. It takes courage to be direct and authentic in your communication, clear and without ambivalence in your convictions, and willing to do what needs to be done. This means that there are days when you won't be the most popular person in the office. It takes courage to make decisions with outcomes that will affect the success of the organization, or to hold firm to your convictions in the face of pressure and opposition.

Courage is about clarity and mindfulness. Courage is not the enforcement of some rigid set of beliefs arbitrarily placed on your followers. Courage is about clarity and mindfulness—clarity as to what you believe and mindfulness in the execution of those beliefs in the culture. It's simple to understand but often hard to implement.

It is the courageous leader who can accept reality as it is and act in alignment with it. Accepting the fact that a favorite long-term employee isn't performing and addressing that issue takes courage. Accepting that there is a conflict between you and another department head and addressing it head-on takes courage. It is the courageous leader who can take responsibility for these choices. Taking responsibility for an error in a forecast and making it right takes courage. Taking responsibility for your part in a dispute and making it right takes courage. Finally, it is the courageous leader who, despite the pressures of the balance sheet, market conditions, and personal gain, will make the decisions that keep people focused on the appropriate values and behaviors. Walking away from a big sale and a big bonus because the customer's business practices are questionable takes courage. Refusing to pad an invoice when all your competitors do so takes courage. Hearing an inappropriate comment and speaking up instead of ignoring it takes courage. The courageous leader makes certain that the organization never loses its ability to focus on the right things at the right time.

It's time for you to move out of your warm, comfortable cocoon and experience the exhilaration of what it's like to lead courageously from the front. Playing it safe will lull you into a false sense of security. The steps in this book will help you break through your barriers and start leading like never before. We will discuss accepting your circumstances and taking responsibility in much greater detail later in the book, but here are five things you can do right now:

1. Clearly identify your core values.

2. Evaluate the extent to which you are leading in alignment with them.

3. Determine if there are areas where you need to be clearer and more direct in communicating and demonstrating those values to your team.

4. Commit to having two conversations in the next week about the implementation and application of those values.

5. Identify an area of your leadership where you are playing it too safe and make a bold, intelligent play.

For a download of a worksheet for this chapter and others please go to www.leadershipisntforcowards.com or scan the QR code.

Leadership Isn't for
Cowards Workbook

CHAPTER 4

Is Culture Overrated?

Now that you've defined your values and the impact you want to have, let's talk about how to use those ideas to influence culture.

Your organization's culture is the way it feels to work there. It is best shown in the stories people tell about you and the way the organization operates. The way customers are treated and how your organization interacts with local communities are also clear indicators of company culture. Do you make it easy for customers to do business with you? Do your employees know that they are respected and appreciated? Culture goes beyond just what it says on some pretty picture posted on the wall. It is about what actually happens every day.

It is pretty simple to be courageous here. You must listen to the stories people are telling about you and your culture, and then you must influence the stories. You must create a space that triggers the kind of story you would be proud to hear at a dinner party.

> You must listen to the stories people are telling about you and your culture, and then you must influence the stories.

What words would make you proudest in the stories your followers tell? Think of four or five words. Categorize them as either scientific or artistic. Which one of the two categories seems more important to you?

Let me share the single most egregious example of cultural failure I have ever experienced. My firm was asked by a CEO to come to his company and help "deepen the outstanding culture." What exactly does that mean? I didn't know then and I don't know now. Our team finally decided that the best way to help them would be to help the leaders identify their core values in order to align the culture with them.

As the morning began, the executives assembled in an off-site conference room. There was a significant amount of skepticism in the air about how effective the meeting would be. In fact, two executives suggested that they just pay us and then take the day off instead.

When we came to the part of the process where the group identified their core values, they chose integrity as their most important core value. As they did, the CEO literally jumped to his feet and said, "That's absolutely ridiculous! There are times when we must violate our integrity in order to close a deal! Integrity will never be a core value of this company!" (I know you're thinking, "Come on, Mike. That didn't really happen!" Unfortunately, it took place *exactly* like that.) After that incident, the meeting immediately ended. Within a month, two top executives left the company.

Now, you might think the point of the story is how bad that CEO is. That's not the point. The CEO defined his values and courageously admitted them, but he did not consider the impact those values would have on the company culture. You need to avoid making the same mistake.

Back in the early to mid-1900s, business required a profoundly different leadership philosophy. Leaders cared only about getting the job done. They weren't as concerned with the human side of business because, frankly, they didn't have to be. But then a plethora of changes took place. Women entered the workplace en masse. Technology took off. Followers demanded clarity from their leaders. Most importantly, people woke up and figured out that the human side of the business was just as important as the numbers side. However, not everyone has accepted the current reality. It is amazing how many leaders still place the P&L before the people. If you are going to be a courageous leader and create a successful business culture, you have to value your human impact and not just your bottom line. Your leader behaviors must clearly demonstrate that.

So what does it take to shape culture?

It takes focus.

Recently I was at an airport and saw a guy carrying on two conversations at the same time, alternating between one cell phone in his right hand and another in his left. I looked at his belt and saw yet another phone. That is not courageous leadership; that is life without boundaries. That is the exact opposite of focus.

I also heard a shocking statistic recently: The average Sunday edition of the *New York Times* has more information in it than the average human being in the 1700s received during his entire lifetime. The speed at which our culture moves—the sheer intensity of the information we must process every day—is beyond overwhelming. If we can't achieve focus and manage the deluge of information that comes at us every day, we'll drown in the chaos. We'll fail to do the things that are most important. We'll fail as leaders.

Remember, leaders work to influence others. If you can't stay focused on your priorities, your followers won't be able to, either. Given the dramatic increase in business speed and information, you won't be able to focus on more than four core centers of excellence. Those things must be the things that are the most important in terms of driving the organization's culture.

That kind of focus takes courage. To whittle away everything that's whizzing and swirling and crashing around you, trying its best to distract you, requires the kind of intense, focused energy that comes from practice. Concentrate on developing your leadership every day, and it will eventually become a habit.

What should be your areas of focus? As an example, a client of mine chose these:

1. Making this the best place to work.

2. Creating an exceptional customer experience.

3. Operational excellence.

4. Financial strength.

How do *you* decide which of your areas of focus? Well, you have to listen.

As a leader, you must start hearing voices! These voices will help you choose your four areas of focus.

1. The voice of your employees/associates:

    By and large, the associates who carry your organization, work group, or team, on their shoulders every day are your best sources of information. They will tell you the truth, if you ask and make it safe for them to be honest. It takes courage on your part. You should be encouraging your people to give you good information on the obstacles in their work. You should be asking them about what it's like to work for you and how you can create a better and more productive culture. (Do not let it turn into a whine festival! The voice of the employee should always be filtered through solutions.) If your employees come to you with a problem, they shouldn't leave your office until they have suggested at least two solutions. A great leader creates a culture in which followers know that problems must be solved and that they must participate in finding the solutions. Challenge your people to give you the truth and to suggest solutions for problems they notice.

2.   The voice of your customer:

For most of our lives we have lived in a provider-driven economy. Basically, the provider of goods and services was in charge of the transaction. Then there came a power shift; we now live in a consumer-driven economy. It is the customer's experience and expectations that drive business. This shift happened because customers have more power—more access and more choices. Listening to what they have to say is not optional if you want to stay in business.

What mechanisms do you have in place to get the voice of the customer loudly in front of you? While surveys are good, it takes even more courage to actually go out and talk with customers face to face. Do not leave this task to your followers alone. Get out there and speak to your clientele. Don't sell to them, listen to them. Find out what they want you to prioritize in your organizational culture.

3.   The voice of your balance sheet:

Have the courage to look deeply into the financials of your area of influence. How are you spending money? Do the expenditures reflect your values?

Let me rephrase that. Your expenditures always reflect your values. Are those expenditures reflective of the kind of culture you want to build? What does the balance sheet say about what you value? What changes do you need to make today? If you don't really have control over your financials, how does that fact reflect your values?

Culture is the heart and soul of your organization. To take it lightly is to risk the long-term success of your leadership. Do not allow yourself to be lulled to sleep by monetary success or market share. Ultimately, it's not the success, but the sustainability of the success, that makes an organization admirable.

> It's not the success, but the sustainability of the success, that makes an organization admirable.

Here are four places to start:

1. Evaluate the extent to which the organization's voices are in balance. Keep in mind that your culture will be a direct reflection of what you value most and the focus you place on any particular voice.

2. If you haven't already, do a professionally administered survey to take the temperature of your current culture. Do not just depend on the stories you hear. It is important to get good, sound evidence.

3. Communicate your four areas of focus to your team. Adjust your leadership behavior to model the culture you want to create around them.

4. Charge your team with eliminating any project or expenditure that distracts you from your four core areas.

For a download of a worksheet for this chapter and others please go to www.leadershipisntforcowards.com or scan the QR code.

Leadership Isn't for
Cowards Workbook

ATTACK

I once read some research that said a huge percentage of what speakers say is forgotten within 48 hours of their saying it. Being a speaker, I took that kind of personally. Every time I spoke for the next couple of months, I thought about that statistic and wondered what I could do to increase how much of my presentations would be retained and used by people.

I came up with an acronym using the word ATTACK. I have used it in hundreds of engagements and have found it helpful for the people to whom I am privileged to speak. I believe you, too, will find it a useful way to remember the important parts of being a courageous leader. The following six sections of this book are each built around one letter of that acronym:

Accept Your Circumstances

Take Action

Take Responsibility

Acknowledge Progress

Commit to New Habits

Kindle

You have already read an introductory section, and when we finish with the acronym I will wrap up with a concluding section. Let's get started!

ACCEPT YOUR CIRCUMSTANCES

The first A in ATTACK stands for *accept your circumstances*. This does not mean that you should envision idealized circumstances and accept that someday they will be reality. Accept your circumstances means facing your situation as it actually is, recognizing your strengths and limitations, and working effectively within your current reality.

Courageous leadership begins with a rigorous acceptance of the truth and the way that truth impacts performance in your followers. Your ability to clearly and wisely accept the circumstances that you are faced with every day will help you solve problems and improve the way your team functions.

CHAPTER 5

How Great Is Denial?

Y ou are in denial when you refuse to accept the reality around you. This reality can include your external situation, the thoughts and feelings you or other people have, and your own capabilities. There is a lot of talk out there about how bad it is to be in denial. Can denial be destructive? Of course it can. Do people destroy themselves and their organizations because of denial? Yes.

There is no doubt that, in at least one area of your life or business, you are in denial. Come on, admit it. If you don't think you are in denial somewhere in your life, then you are in denial about being in denial. So make it easy on yourself and just admit it. You may be in denial about how poorly your department is doing. You may be in denial about the negative effects of your favorite junk food. Those are examples of destructive denial. Destructive denial is when you refuse to accept reality, and that refusal clearly has destructive consequences.

> **If you don't think you are in denial somewhere in your life, then you are in denial about being in denial.**

But perhaps it's not always so bad. Is there a place for denial? Are there times when denial is your ally and a method to reach goals in spite of challenging circumstances? Are there times that it can be used for good, to achieve great things?

I believe so. I have experienced it personally and I've read story after story in which denial, used effectively, served as a driver. Before you get nervous about my promoting some kind of delusional way of leading, consider the rest of this chapter.

Years ago, I had a grad school instructor who said, "Do not strip denial away from your clients. For some, that's all they have."

Denial can help people press courageously forward into formidable circumstances, and in some cases it can enable them to create success. They simply refuse to accept their limitations and move in without acknowledging the difficulties around them. For some, it allows them to go day to day, week to week, month to month, year to year, achieving results in the face of challenging situations. A manager has a team with minimal talent, but they achieve remarkable success. An athlete is told in his youth that he lacks the skill to play his favorite sport, but he goes on to achieve international recognition as one of the best athletes of all time. A musician supposedly does not have the coordination necessary to perform but becomes one of the most skilled instrumentalists ever to play in a concert hall. Most triumphantly, a patient is told she has stage four cancer with little chance of survival and pushes through to beat the disease. Denial is not always a bad thing.

The beauty of denial is that you, as a coach or leader, can use it to your benefit. Let's say you're trying to get a project completed and you know that you don't have the people to do it the way it needs to be done. The leader without courage would give the team some half-hearted encouragement, leaving them with doubt and depleted energy. The courageous leader, despite the limitations, would challenge his followers to believe the project would work and to act accordingly.

Denial is constructive when you press on, not in some cheesy psychobabble way, but in a way that inspires achievement against all odds. The leader has to dream bigger than the followers. The leader has to see what the followers can't see and push them forward in spite of reality.

> **The leader has to see what the followers can't see and push them forward in spite of reality.**

History is full of stories about how denial helped create amazing accomplishments. It is easy to believe that those people and organizations are somehow gifted or uniquely talented, but often that is not the case.

In the early 1900s, a young boy named Glenn Cunningham was severely injured in a school fire. He lost all the toes on his left foot. The flesh on his knees and shins was destroyed. His right leg was severely deformed and healed two inches shorter than his left. His legs were so badly injured that he lost the function in them. He and his parents were told that he would probably never walk again and would certainly be disabled for the rest of his life. In fact, the doctors recommended amputation. His mother refused.

While sitting outside one day, Glenn pushed himself out of his wheelchair, fell to the ground, and dragged himself to a fence post. There, he pulled himself up and began dragging himself along the fence. He did this every day until he began to walk.

More amazingly, he discovered that while it hurt to walk, it didn't hurt when he ran. He baffled doctors, family, and friends as he ran the country roads of Kansas. He went on to set world records as a college track star.

He is a great example of how denial can be a powerful tool when used appropriately. The doctors told him and his family that there was no hope, but he denied that supposed reality and was rewarded for it.

This concept applies to more than athletics. You could argue that Martin Luther King Jr. was denying the presence of impossible circumstances when he spoke of achieving civil rights that few really believed were possible. John F. Kennedy denied the near impossible challenges that were present when he said we would land on the moon in ten years. More recently, Steve Jobs denied the conventional wisdom when he co-founded Pixar and went on to turn it into an amazing success story. And you, if you thought about it long enough (and you should), could think of a time in your own life when you denied something and succeeded in spite of the obstacles.

Athlete, advocate, or business leader, it makes little difference. You know people who have denied the odds and achieved amazing results despite their circumstances. Courage requires that you be willing to suffer or fail in the pursuit of that which matters most to you and your followers. Sometimes you have to deny reality to maintain that courage.

> Courage requires that you be willing to suffer or fail in the pursuit of that which matters most to you and your followers.

By this point you must be thinking, "Hold it, hold it! I thought this section was about *accepting*. How can you accept your circumstances and still be in denial?"

That is a great question. The useful thing about denial is that you can deny the power of the obstacle while still accepting its existence. You can look at it as it actually is but refuse to let it overpower you, even if it seems like you can't avoid it.

Denial can help you minimize the relentless excuse-making in which many people engage. People often use excuses to avoid action. Denial in this context refuses to let the presence of the obstacle define the outcome. Acknowledging the presence of the obstacle but denying its power can build powerful momentum. This requires the adoption of a "what; so, what" mentality. With the "what" you ask yourself, "What are the actual circumstances?" The "so, what" requires even more thought. It prompts you to ask yourself, "*So, what* are we going to do about it?" Denying the presence of the obstacle is just plain delusional. Denying that it will defeat you or limit you is just plain courageous.

Your followers deserve a leader who will openly accept the presence of obstacles, challenges, and even tragedies, but deny their power and refuse to succumb, even if most people believe they mean certain defeat. Courageous leadership is grounded in the belief that accepting your circumstances is not equal to surrendering to them. Accepting that the economy is struggling is not equal to surrendering to poor performance. Accepting that you have high turnover is not surrendering to it and letting it sidetrack and discourage you. Accepting that you are sick doesn't mean refusing the appropriate treatment.

So consider your leadership in the light of denial. Think about where you may be allowing circumstances to define you and limit your influence. It takes huge amounts of energy to deny the power of your circumstances. You can't sell your direct reports on an idea that is not based in reality, but you can stand in front of them and, while you acknowledge the obstacles in your way, deny their power over you. Do this, and your influence will increase significantly. It will increase because your direct reports will rally behind you. It will increase because they will trust you when you show your faith in them. It will increase because they will support you and finally, because it will inspire them to do more and do better.

Here are four ideas to get you started:

1. Identify your areas of denial and then evaluate whether those areas are constructive or destructive to maintain.

2. Commit to a communication strategy that fully and completely acknowledges the reality of your circumstances.

3. Point out the wins in achieving your goals and objectives. Keep the focus on the wins without paying too much attention to the losses.

4. What are you allowing to limit you and how would denying its power help you achieve more and lead better?

For a download of a worksheet for this chapter and others please go to www.leadershipisntforcowards.com or scan the QR code.

Leadership Isn't for
Cowards Workbook

CHAPTER 6

What Are You Pretending Not to Know?

That is one of the best questions I have ever been asked: What are you pretending not to know?

Most people go through life with some level of pretending. Our earliest childhood games involved pretending, and those games helped us learn to interact with each other and the world. Childhood pretending has many positive effects.

Interestingly enough, adult pretending tends to have a negative impact. It can actually diminish your self-esteem and erode your credibility. You know from your own experiences that it causes problems when you pretend things are different than they are. It is likely that you've worked for a person who pretended not to know things, looked the other way when problems occurred, or acted in a way that didn't align with what you knew was true. It probably made it challenging to maintain a healthy level of respect for that person.

In the previous chapter, we looked at the power of denial and how that denial can help you be effective. Here, we'll explore how your own pretending or the pretending of your followers can limit effectiveness. For the purposes of leadership, pretending is acting as if something exists, or does not exist, when you know deep in your core that the opposite is true.

So how does pretending differ from denial? The biggest difference is that pretending means you know something but act as if you don't. You can pretend not to know both positive things and negative things. You can act as if you don't know about opportunities in order to avoid risk. You can pretend you don't know about problems to avoid holding people accountable. Denial is about suppressing unhelpful information and denying its power; pretending is about acting as if that information didn't exist.

Pretending is common in the workplace. I have found that most leaders either overestimate or underestimate the health of their current culture and the effectiveness of the people who work in it. Very few people have a realistic grasp on their situation. As a leader, you need to look reality in the face and accept it. So why do so many leaders act as if something is or is not real when in fact they are aware, at some level, of the truth?

> As a leader, you need to look reality in the face and accept it.

The fact of the matter is that examining the truth in the full light of reality triggers behavioral and emotional impulses that we would prefer to ignore. If the doctor tells you that you need to lose weight or you are going to have a heart attack, it doesn't feel good and it should trigger better dietary behaviors—behaviors you would prefer not to change. If your employee feedback survey comes back with less than desirable results, it may trigger anger or disappointment. It may trigger a search for a coach or discussions with groups of followers to see what can be changed. None of that is particularly pleasant. Ignoring reality can make us feel better in the short run and can increase positive feelings. The avoidance of pain and the pursuit of pleasure are both at the top of the list of human motivations. Human beings will do more to reduce pain than almost anything else.

People will often say, "Oh no, pain doesn't motivate me, this other thing does." That's interesting—wrong, but interesting. For example, let's say you and I have known each other for years, and from the beginning of our friendship, you've told me about how much money motivates you. "Oh, if I just had more money, my life would be better!" So one day I show up with $900,000 and say, "Here you go. It's yours." Then as you reach for it, I say, "Not so fast! Before I give you that money, you must sit on the hot burner on your stove for thirty seconds!"

If you are like 100 percent of my audiences, you would say, "There is no way I'm sitting on that red hot burner, even for thirty seconds! The pain is too much."

See? While the money is appealing, it's not worth the pain. Most people won't willingly endure significant pain, even for a reward. When pain increases in our circumstances, we make changes to reduce it. Until the pain exceeds the fear of change, nobody really does anything.

No, I am not suggesting that you should inflict pain to provoke change. I'm suggesting that the reason so many people refuse to turn on the lights of reality is that they would rather delay or eliminate the pain that reality would cause.

You may have a person working for you and you are pretending not to know that their time with your organization is over. Maybe their current capabilities don't match the needs of their job, but they're a nice person and they always pitch in where they can, so you allow them to stay. Maybe you are pretending not to know that your behavior is having a negative impact on those who follow you.

On a positive note, maybe you are pretending not to know how significant your influence is in the organization. Instead of using it, you stay quiet. Maybe you are pretending not to know that your time with your company is over. Better yet, maybe you should be asking for a promotion or a raise.

Maybe you are pretending not to know that your team is functioning at a very high level; for whatever reason, you continue to ride them and correct them and find fault with them.

Maybe you know that a difficult conversation needs to be had, but the uncomfortable feelings associated with the idea cause you to avoid it.

Many times, we put things off or pretend not to know about them because it's just plain easier . . . for now.

Eliminating pretending as an organizational or personal strategy is a critical step to leading courageously. But, as you can imagine, it's not easy. It's not supposed to be.

> Eliminating pretending as an organizational or personal strategy is a critical step to leading courageously.

You already know what you need to do, so stop pretending and go do it!

Here are four steps to get you started:

1. Focus your energy on listening to the voices mentioned in Chapter 4 (the employees, the customer, and the financial statement). What facts do they convey? Which ones have you been pretending not to know?

2. Listen to neutral sources of information, people without biases. What do they say about your reality?

3. Find a person that you trust. Have them ask you tough questions and respectfully deliver the real truth to you.

4. Most importantly: What are you pretending not to know about yourself that is positive? What are you pretending not to know about your team that is positive?

For a download of a worksheet for this chapter and others please go to www.leadershipisntforcowards.com or scan the QR code.

Leadership Isn't for
Cowards Workbook

CHAPTER 7

Are You Honest?

Someone somewhere once said, "Honesty is always the best policy." Really? Have you ever thought through the implications of that statement?

Ever had a person say something to you that was hurtful, unkind, or offensive? You ask them why they would say something like that and they answer, "I'm just being honest!" You probably want to respond, "Well, lie a little!"

People often confuse honesty with strong opinions—with something that they believe but that is not really *true*. I would like you to consider honesty from a different perspective.

Some years back, I was encouraged by a friend to go on a blind date. I have always had a policy against blind dates. They seldom work out well and the person setting me up always seems to lead with, "She has a great personality."

My friend's persuasiveness was capped with, "Look, Mike, your dating life is a desert. Just give it a try." Reluctantly, I agreed to go out with his friend. We seemed to have some things in common, and she was attractive, too, based on the pictures we had exchanged online. All looked like a go.

I arrived at her home to pick her up, and when she came to the door . . . let's just say she didn't look exactly like her picture. Nevertheless, we had a nice evening with great conversation, but it became clear there was no second date in our future. There just wasn't much chemistry, and neither of us was "feeling it."

On the way home, she asked the one question no man wants to be asked. Drum roll, please! She asked me, "Can I ask you a question?" Every man knows that when that question is asked, whatever comes next is going to be a test for which he hasn't studied. After I agreed, she asked, "Do you think I look like my picture?"

Uh oh. My mind flew through answers until I finally landed on a good choice. Certain that I had found the answer that would keep me out of trouble, I said, "You know, a picture only captures a person in one moment in time. It doesn't give you a full sense of how they look. That can only happen when you meet them in person."

She seemed to accept that, and then asked me another question. "Do you want to know what I thought of your picture?"

I said, "No, not really!"

Then, with full conviction, she told me, "When I saw your picture, I thought you were really good-looking, but now that I've met you in person, you look really old, tired, and worn-out!"

I then said, "Have you ever been pushed out of a speeding European automobile?"

Just kidding. What I did say was, "Why would you say something like that?"

She said, "I was just being honest."

Now, there is no need to write to me with your opinion on whether or not she was right. The point is that she believed she was communicating truth when she was simply stating her opinion. As hard as it is for many to believe, opinions are not necessarily truth. Your opinions may be the truth *as you see it*, but they aren't universal in their accuracy. So if you are serious about being courageous and influencing others in significant ways, then it will help you to take a second look at how you employ honesty.

> As hard as it is for many to believe, opinions are not necessarily truth.

Honesty is the best policy *only* when it meets these three criteria:

1. Factual accuracy

2. Usefulness for the listener

3. Constructive delivery

We'll look at these one at a time.

FACTUAL ACCURACY

In order for something to be true, it must be based on facts. Leaders must take seriously what they say and how they say it. While comments casually spoken when you are not a leader might have little effect, the same comments made from a position of power can have a massive impact. Consider carefully the extent to which what you are about to say is factually accurate and can be supported with objective data.

> Comments casually spoken when you are not a leader might have little effect, the same comments made from a position of power can have a massive impact.

It may be factually accurate to say, "Our first quarter sales numbers are off by 10 percent, and that has to change immediately." The trouble starts when you add, "And you were lazy this quarter." I am not suggesting that opinions have no place, but presenting opinions and subjective judgments as facts is not honest and will likely stir up defensiveness in listeners.

It takes courage to speak the facts and own your opinions. If you want to voice an opinion, then go ahead, but make sure you communicate it as just that—your opinion. If you want to really stretch yourself, then state a fact and ask a question by saying something like, "Sales were off by 10 percent. I would like to know why." This strategy will create more honest space for discussion.

USEFULNESS FOR THE LISTENER

Even if your facts are accurate, there is no need to share them if your followers can't use them. More trivial information is shared in meetings and reviews than can ever be assimilated and applied to improve performance. If you share tons of data that doesn't have a direct use in helping your followers increase efficiency or drive results, then I beg you to stop sharing it. Stop forcing them to sit in dark rooms with irrelevant, font-too-small PowerPoint presentations. Stop droning on about information that you find immensely interesting but doesn't help them do their jobs better. When you give a performance review, be certain that your conversation is fact-based and packed with useful information. You want the people you influence to leave with

> You want the people you influence to leave with immediately applicable, completely usable data that will help them do more of what is necessary and less of what is not.

immediately applicable, completely usable data that will help them do more of what is necessary and less of what is not.

CONSTRUCTIVE DELIVERY

A message may be factually accurate and useful to the listener, but delivered in such a way that it becomes destructive in its impact. The courageous communicator can effectively deliver a message that's constructive, direct, firm, and respectful all at once, helping to improve performance and promoting further development and advancement.

I know, I know, some of you are thinking, "I'm not into all that warm and fuzzy stuff. I call it as I see it, and they just need to take it and get back to work." Take it easy there, Captain Kindness. This is not about warm and fuzzy. It's about delivering a message in the most effective way possible so that you achieve results quicker and with better long-term effects on your followers. Phrase things constructively, and you will earn constructive results.

So, is honesty the best policy? That depends on your commitment to making your communication factual, useful, and constructive.

Much destruction has been brought about by the careless, even reckless ways some leaders communicate the "truth." Accepting things as they actually are does not necessarily mean slamming the truth down everyone else's throats. Nor does it mean, as we discussed in Chapter 6, pretending the truth is not the truth. Courage in this context involves delivering authentic messages in ways that those around you can *use*. You still get to communicate your opinions and ideas; just make sure you qualify them as what they are, keeping in mind that what you say has a tremendous impact on the people who follow you.

Are you honest? Answering that question is the point of this chapter. The answer lies in how well you deliver on the three criteria we have discussed.

Here's how to make honesty the best policy in your leadership:

1. On a scale of 0 to 10 (0 if you're terrible at it, 10 if you're perfect at it), score yourself on how well you manage each of the three traits of effective honesty: factual, useful, and constructive. If you gave yourself 10s on each of them, you aren't being honest. Want proof? Ask your direct reports.

2. Choose one of the three to focus on improving over the next 90 days.

3. Be courageous, tell the truth, and commit to authenticity, but modify your delivery for your audience based on the three traits in this chapter.

For a download of a worksheet for this chapter and others please go to www.leadershipisntforcowards.com or scan the QR code.

Leadership Isn't for
Cowards Workbook

CHAPTER 8

What Is Real?

How's that for a deep question? There's no need to explore the deepest philosophical reaches of the universe to answer it, though. Reality is factual, not perceptual. Reality is the state of things as they actually exist, as opposed to an idealistic or perceived state. Despite whatever clichés might be floating around out there, reality is not hard to figure out. Once the emotions, opinions, and other distractions are stripped away, reality is left.

> Once the emotions, opinions, and other distractions are stripped away, reality is left.

Being courageous as a leader involves a rigorous commitment to accept reality. Section II of this book has been entirely committed to acceptance—to an understanding of your circumstances and how you can leverage them in your leadership without surrendering to them. To do that, you first have to know what your reality is.

There are two kinds of reality: the current reality and the desired future reality. Both are straightforward, but many leaders lose sight of these two important realities when it comes to day-to-day decisions.

The current reality is the reality that is right here, right now, in this moment. It is the factual representation of the current state of being for the circumstances you are in. It is the way things are right now, without any emotional or subjective bias. Your current reality forces you to focus on what is, without making mountains out of molehills or vice versa.

While it seems simple and obvious here in black and white, it is much harder to execute this focus in your leadership behavior. Your emotional bias generally colors reality in a way that makes the most sense given the emotion through which it is seen. If you are very excited about a proposal you have written, you are likely to see only the great things about that proposal while overlooking its weaknesses. If you are in love, you are likely to see only the great things about your partner and rationalize away their flaws or irritating habits. If you are angry with a direct report, you are most likely to see only those things that reinforce your anger. You have probably made an emotional purchase at one time or another—you know, those times when you go to the local big-box store, get all excited about something, buy it, get it home, and then think, "Why did I buy a turbo weed whacker? I live in a condo!" It is challenging to see reality clearly when emotion is involved, but your acceptance of your current reality must be free of emotional bias in order to be useful.

This is not to suggest that emotional bias is a bad thing; an emotional bias toward caring about the well-being of people you influence is a healthy and appropriate thing to have, for example. In Chapter 7, we talked about how strong opinions sometimes seem like truth. Your bias is what causes that. Everyone has emotional biases, and awareness of that fact can help you understand why other people see the world the way they do. You can accept the various ways people interpret what you say, and then communicate more effectively. The point is not to eliminate your bias, but rather to understand it and suspend it when looking at reality.

Take a step back and consider: How much of your view of your current reality is clear and without emotional bias? How much of it is based on your own subjective perceptions? Those questions can be difficult to answer. Find a person whose judgment is not altered and ask them to help you with clarity.

I laugh when I hear people say, "Perception is reality." No, it's not. Reality is concrete; it doesn't matter what your perception is. If perception was reality, then anything you perceive would be real, which is clearly not the case. If it were, I could perceive that I looked like Matthew McConaughey, and—*poof!*—my perception would be real.

That is clearly not the case. However, a person can live as if all of their perceptions were their reality; in fact, many people do. They live as though everything they perceive is true, regardless of whether or not the real world agrees. We call them crazy people.

It requires courage to stare reality in the face and encourage those you lead to do the same. Biased perceptions, like pretending, are comfortable. Reality is not scary, in and of itself. It is not exciting in and of itself, either. Reality finds its impact in the meaning we give it. We are each the star of our own story; we build narratives about our current realities and then act in alignment with the conclusions we've drawn.

> It requires courage to stare reality in the face and encourage those you lead to do the same.

Because of the way your perceptions impact your actions, it is critical that your leader behaviors focus on your current reality as it really is. Your view of reality will affect your impact, so make sure your view is clear and accurate.

Future reality is a bit of an oxymoron. Unless you have recently been certified as a reliable fortune teller, it is very hard to perceive much less know the future. So instead, establish with your team a picture of the *desirable* reality of the future. Though five-year business plans are dinosaurs, it is useful to agree on words and phrases that clearly describe your desired future reality. They should be easily measurable when you arrive at the specified point in the future, such as "profitable," "debt-free," and "low employee turnover."

Courageous leadership, based in reality, will take your followers far beyond their current beliefs about their capabilities and into the desired future reality. However, that can only happen when you, as their leader, help them see the facts of the current reality without attaching bias.

Here are three suggestions to help you lead from reality:

1. Teach your direct reports to communicate factually before they add bias to their reports or discussions. Strive to do the same.

2. Communicate early and often about the circumstances of your current reality so that you are never caught unaware.

3. Work with your team to envision your desired future reality. How can you get there, based on your current reality?

For a download of a worksheet for this chapter and others please go to www.leadershipisntforcowards.com or scan the QR code.

Leadership Isn't for
Cowards Workbook

CHAPTER 9

Where Is Your Focus?

We've touched on focus in earlier chapters, but how do you actually do it? Focus is one of the biggest challenges for a leader. While some reading this may believe that they are perfectly focused, most will admit that they can't possibly deal with all of the demands facing them. Whether you are a CEO or a frontline supervisor, your energy is a precious resource, and an inability to focus on the right thing at the right time with the right amount of intensity will decrease the effectiveness of your leadership.

There is a ratio between how much energy you invest in any given demand of your day and the kind of return you get on that investment. Sharpening your focus will increase the likelihood that your organization will perform at the highest level.

Unfortunately, many people (and you know who you are) tend to overestimate their capacity. The American work ethic had always suggested that the harder you worked, the more successful you were. Then somebody came along and told us that we should *work smarter*, managing our time carefully. Really? Work smarter? That implies we have been working dumber all this time, and I don't agree with that. In fact, I don't think it's about working harder or smarter at all. I don't even think it's about time management. I think it's about getting the highest rate of return on the *energy* you invest on a daily basis.

It's time to come to terms with the fact that you simply can't do it all. It's the truth. (I would also suggest that it's time to realize that you can't make everybody happy, and that's okay.)

So what are you focused on? Things that will have the most profitable and productive

> **It's time to come to terms with the fact that you simply can't do it all.**

47

impact on your organization? Things that will create success for those that follow you? Things that drive high-impact performance? Or all of the above and a thousand other things, too?

It takes courage to be disciplined and focus on the things that will have the greatest impact, as opposed to the things that make you feel the busiest. Many people say they are busy at work, but they are not actually productive.

Let's assume you have good intentions and that you want your followers to succeed and win. Let's also assume your followers have good intentions and that most of them want to succeed and win. If all that is true, then why is it so hard for people to focus? Why are distractions so, well, distracting? We all seem to have what a friend of mine calls the shiny ball syndrome: You are hard at work when a shiny ball rolls by. You get up and chase it, forgetting what you're supposed to be doing. Focus is within your grasp for a time, but in the long run, it escapes. The shiny ball comes in many forms, including emails, texts, phone calls, and less urgent tasks that tug at your attention. It could be remembering an errand you need to run or a proposal you need to write. The shiny ball is anything that distracts you.

For most of us, focus escapes because we don't have the courage to say no. Since we were kids, we have been taught to study harder, run further, work longer, and get more done. By the time we are adults, we have an ever-growing checklist of responsibilities and tasks and errands, and we can't focus on any of it.

My buddy, Brian, invited me to Charlotte, North Carolina, for the NASCAR Nationwide Race on Memorial Day weekend. He got me a pit pass, no less. I had never been to a NASCAR event, so I wasn't sure what to expect.

Prior to the race, we stood in a car hauler talking to a driver and his crew chief. I asked the driver where he qualified to start. "Twenty-seventh," he said. (For a rookie driver to start 27th in a field of 43 is a big deal.) I asked, "How many seconds faster was the person starting first?" He said it wasn't seconds; it was tenths of a second. Those tenths of a second could equal millions of dollars in prize money.

After that, we went to the parts area where they showed us springs, shocks, and many other tiny parts that I couldn't identify (to tell you the truth, I couldn't identify most of the large ones either). I was told that those tenths of a second that allowed the other driver to start first were shaved off by reducing weight and drag on the car (and also, obviously, by having a great driver and engine). So the weight of each of those little parts mattered—the weight added drag, and drag cost lots of money. I was struck by how such small, unnoticeable changes could make a difference of millions of dollars.

Weight and drag, weight and drag, weight and drag, rang through my head all day as I watched 43 cars, each with 800 horsepower, fly around the track. Engines blew out, cars got lapped, and one driver won. It was a level of exhilaration I have seldom experienced!

So where is your weight and drag? What are you holding onto that, if you let it go, would increase your personal or professional performance? Do you have the courage to clearly identify three or four things that create weight and drag in your work environment? Is there a meeting that has been sacred for years but needs to go? Is there a policy that needs to be eliminated? Where can you make small adjustments to increase your focus? Can you lead your team to let go of those things?

I have yet to see an organization that could not get rid of some weight and drag. Maybe it's a policy, a person, a scarcity mindset, or any number of other things that drag your productivity down. For instance, at some retail stores any employee can authorize returns, while many other retailers require managerial approval. Of course, the managers almost always approve the returns. Taking the time to call a manager is drag; it's weight on the brand's reputation, and it implies to the customer that the employees cannot be trusted to make decisions. Worse yet, it implies to the employees that management doesn't trust them. Maybe you require your staff to jump through certain approval processes or spend a certain amount of time in the office or take lunch at specific times when it doesn't affect the results of the department at all. Maybe they are focused on activities that add weight and drag to their jobs. Maybe you mandate that focus; if so it's time to reduce some of that weight and drag on your followers. I am certain it is costing you a lot of money.

Let's wrap up this chapter by making the question of focus more about you. What are you doing or not doing that is adding weight and drag? Are you refusing to make a decision,

> It's time to reduce some of that weight and drag on your followers.

waiting to hire an assistant, delaying a hiring or firing issue, or spending time doing something inefficient? Whatever the source of drag in your work, it is critical that you make small adjustments to control it.

At the core of your job is your role as obstacle remover. Like the traffic reporter flying in a helicopter above the highway, examining where the flow of traffic is slow, you must look clearly and constantly at the flow of productivity in your group. Your job is to get out in front of your followers and aggressively fight for the removal of obstacles in their paths. If you can control it, do it today. If you can't remove it yourself, but have access to those who can, lobby for change. If there is nothing that can be done, coach your people in the most effective way to cope and succeed in spite of it. Be courageous: Remove the obstacles you can and work around the ones that remain so that you can stay productive, directed, and focused.

> **At the core of your job is your role as obstacle remover.**

Here are three steps to help you get started:

1. Determine where you lack focus. What is one small adjustment you can make that would reduce drag?

2. Ask each of those you lead to identify one specific thing that increases weight and drag, and then encourage them to eliminate it or, if they can't do it themselves, eliminate it for them.

3. Evaluate your team, by person. What's the best use of each person's energy? What needs to happen for them to radically increase their focus on those areas?

For a download of a worksheet for this chapter and others please go to www.leadershipisntforcowards.com or scan the QR code.

Leadership Isn't for
Cowards Workbook

SECTION 3

TAKE ACTION

The first T in ATTACK stands for *take action*. Delaying action can, at best, limit leadership effectiveness; at worst, delaying action is paralyzing. In this section, we will help you build a balance between being ready and taking risks. We will explore how to balance your gut with your analysis while still making things happen. You will clearly see where you can make adjustments to increase your action orientation.

CHAPTER 10

Are You Good at Analyzing?

If you have been in leadership for any period of time, you have probably become a decent analyzer. Analysis is about examining, scrutinizing, studying, investigating, and evaluating. The ability to analyze helps you solve problems, make decisions, and generally keep your organization on track. Whatever score-keeping method or metrics you use, I'm sure you leverage your analysis in a way that drives results.

The question is: Do you use your analytical capabilities to courageously make decisions and reduce behaviors that do not support the results you want?

"Are you good at analyzing?" is a yes or no question. It boxes you in. There is a reason for that cornering; while your analytical skills are most likely good (if they aren't, I am sorry to tell you that this book isn't going to help with that), it is equally likely that your utilization of that analysis needs work. You either are or are not a good analyzer, hence the question, but it's what you do with the data and information you analyze that makes you a good leader. That subject is more complicated.

Most people think analysis is strictly on the scientific side of your leadership. They see it as a cold, calculated evaluation of numbers, strategies, and formulas. For some leaders, analysis is also a process that allows them to pretend (and remember that pretending is a bad thing) that they are busy and delay decisions. Yeah, yeah, I know, you have to do good analysis before you can make a decision. The topic here is more expansive than just analyzing.

It goes to the word *good*. Good analysis can be applied in multiple settings. It can be used as an art as much as a science. It can be used to analyze things that don't fit so nicely into the boxes that true analysts love to create. A *good* analyzer can analyze any situation on multiple levels without having to rely on a set series of tricks and tools. Recently, I was in a meeting with some people who were planning a conference. About halfway through the meeting, one guy said, "I've got a great idea! Let's take the total number of minutes in the conference, divide by the number of learning objectives, then create a spreadsheet . . ." As the room collectively fell into a coma, he also suggested a complete analysis of the attendees' demographics, the conference hours, the color of the venue's carpet . . . you get the idea. He became rather upset as the group resisted his desire to analyze. Resisted is a nice way of saying it. The truth is, they rolled their eyes and blew him off, basically ignoring anything else he had to say.

No doubt he was a good analyzer. In fact, some of his ideas would have probably helped the team plan a better conference. But here's the deal: People that don't like analysis and aren't good at it find it *painful*. The other team members resisted the idea of analysis because they couldn't stand doing it!

> **Courageous leaders must merge their scientific and artistic sides to perform good analysis.**

Analyzing can be scary because courageous analysis requires the combination of two things: First, the realities of the facts, and second, the voice of your gut, or intuition. Courageous leaders must merge their scientific and artistic sides to perform good analysis. They can not only look at the data, analyze the facts, and draw reasonable conclusions, but are also able to mix these findings with a check of the gut. It takes both your head and your gut to make you a good analyzer. For people who prefer one over the other, that's intimidating.

Most people look at the gut and the head as opposites. They're right. However, courageous leaders work to balance those opposites; they understand that decisions that have a direct impact on people's lives require both the head and the gut. Here's the good news: You do not need to reduce your reliance on facts and data to increase your reliance on your gut, and you do not need to reduce your reliance on your gut to increase your attention to facts.

This also applies to decisions made by the people you are leading. I am constantly amazed at how many people will tell a direct report,

"Stop worrying so much about the facts and make a gut decision!" In other cases, I hear, "Quit that intuitive decision-making! Focus on the facts!" As if one were more effective than the other. In truth, neither is better or worse; both are necessary to drive results. Your leadership will be enhanced, the performance of your team will improve, and they will likely trust you more if you lead with both your head and your gut. They are like two sides of the same coin, and the extent to which you have them work together will enhance the effectiveness of your leadership.

One challenge emerges when the leader is more comfortable with one side of the coin and the follower is more comfortable with the other. When you have someone working for you who is a logic-driven, fact-based performer, and you are an intuitive leader who likes the fact that not everything fits in a spreadsheet, conflicts can emerge. Fear not! You don't need to get annoyed or get that follower to shift to your way of seeing the world.

Consider this: It is easier to start thinking about something than to stop. Try it. Start thinking about the ocean. Go ahead; just consider it your mid-book relaxation exercise. I won't tell anyone you took a little breather. Bring pictures of the ocean to your mind. Imagine the smell of the ocean, the sound of the ocean, the feel of the wind of the ocean. Get a vivid picture and imagine real sensations.

Now, with that image and thought in your head, try to stop thinking about the ocean. Repeat to yourself, "I am not going to think about the ocean. I must eliminate the thought of the ocean from my mind. I will stop thinking about the ocean."

If you were able to remove the ocean from your mind, you probably did so by adding something else to your thinking. You began thinking about another topic to take your mind off the ocean. You didn't really stop thinking about the ocean; you began thinking about something else. The same strategy works for balancing the scales between logic and intuition. When you are working with direct reports to drive performance or solve a problem, don't try to convince them to see it your way. It won't work. Instead, validate their ways of seeing it (you don't necessarily have to agree with them) and then to ask them to verify it with the other side. If one is convinced at a gut level that something is the right move, ask for an analysis of the facts to see how closely it supports the intuition. If, on the other hand, a follower is all about the facts, then ask that the data be put aside to allow for consideration of what their gut is saying. In both instances, you are likely to meet resistance. We all like to use the type of decision-making we are most comfortable with, but this method will be much more effective than trying to take away a follower's favorite way of problem solving.

So what about you? How exactly are you supposed to learn to balance the facts with your gut? (No doubt you are more comfortable looking at things from one side or the other.) If things need to make sense to you, you are likely more comfortable with your head. If things need to feel right to you, then your gut is dominant.

If you prefer facts over intuition:

1. Before you begin to analyze the facts, look at the problem you need to solve or the decision you need to make and write down what you think the answer is. Put that aside and forget about it.

2. Then, go investigate, evaluate, make spreadsheets, and dig up information to your heart's content. Do everything you need to do to look at the facts, then write down your decision or solution.

3. Take out the first piece of paper and compare your gut decision to your fact-based decision. How similar are they? While some people have naturally good intuition, others don't. If your gut decision is nothing like your factual decision, don't worry. Your intuition can be developed like a muscle; it just needs practice.

4. Continue to repeat this exercise until an inconsequential decision or issue presents itself. Then, be courageous by making a 100 percent gut-based decision.

If you prefer your gut over facts or logic:

1. Resist the urge to say "I can already tell you what the answer is even before I get into all this." Set aside your gut instinct and ignore it.

2. Before making a decision, investigate. Search out every available fact and see what decision the data alone supports.

3. If you find this challenging, find an über-logical person who asks good questions and can help you to analyze logically.

4. Compare your original gut instinct to your data-based conclusion. Are they the same or different? Why or why not?

Keep in mind that these are the same steps to use with those you influence. Remember that the goal is to have equal measure of both parts, and while you may have a tendency or a preference toward logic and facts over your gut, or vice versa, work diligently to balance both.

For a download of a worksheet for this chapter and others please go to www.leadershipisntforcowards.com or scan the QR code.

Leadership Isn't for
Cowards Workbook

CHAPTER 11

When Are You Ready?

Please stop short of answering that question with "Well, you just know!" As I hope you realize by now, if you tried to say that, I would jump off the pages of this book and shake you! (I wish the laws of metaphysics made it that easy.)

There are only two, maybe three, types of leaders in my experience: First, there are gunslingers who make gut decisions on the fly; second, there are those who love to mull over the facts and data; and finally, there are those who balance both. So, assuming you have managed to balance the two sides, as was suggested in the previous chapter, how do you know when you are ready to take action?

So many times, leaders and organizations spend too much time getting ready to be ready to get ready to almost get ready to be ready to get ready. Then, they form a committee or a task force (which is just a committee on steroids) to evaluate more and look into the situation more so that they can *really* be ready. Just how much getting ready does a leader need? What makes you think that if you are a little more ready, you are going to get results that are *so much* better?

You say, "But Mike, you emphasized at the beginning of this book that we are messing with people's lives! Shouldn't we take our time and make sure we are ready before we take action?" Great question. The answer is . . . well, sort of. Here's the deal: You should know that taking too much time getting ready burns valuable resources and drags the organization down all kinds of inefficient alleys. Naturally, you don't want to do that. So how much is enough?

I would suggest that getting overly ready is a result of fear and not courage. You don't want to fail, so instead you put off the moment of truth by perpetually getting ready. Should you prepare? Of course. Do your research? Yes. But stop hiding behind the we-aren't-quite-ready curtain. Say, "Enough is enough," and take action!

Today, more than ever, we are faced with an unprecedented speed of change. The world, including the corporate world, is moving faster than it ever has, and waiting until you are completely ready will quickly destroy opportunities. One of the most courageous things you can do for those you lead is to shift them from a waiting mindset to an anticipating, action-based mindset. Agility and quickness are no longer options; they are mandates. The consumer demands it, technology demands it, and your direct reports demand it (though they may not tell you so). If you want to drain the energy right out of an organization, hold onto the belief that being ready is some magical state in which all the t's are crossed, all the i's are dotted, and the risk is nil. If you wait for that, you'll be waiting a long time. Messy and quick is better than perfect and slow. Followers need to see their leaders boldly charge forward with purpose and conviction.

> **Messy and quick is better than perfect and slow.**

One night, I was traveling on an evening flight, and about an hour in, the captain came on the PA system and said, "Ladies and gentlemen, this is your captain. I need you to please listen to me right now!" Now, I don't know about you, but I seldom listen to anything said over the PA, with the exception of the destination's weather, but the intensity in the captain's voice perked me right up. He continued, "We are about to fly into very rough air. In fact, the air is so rough, it is likely to make you very uncomfortable, so I am going to ask the flight attendants to take their seats." So far, pretty routine. Then he said, "This rough air is going to last about ten minutes, and it's going to be *very* rough. The second officer and I have over fifty years of experience between the two of us, and the airplane is built to handle much worse than this. So between our experience and this plane's design, you will be safe at all times, even though it may not *feel* that way. It's going to last about ten minutes, then it will be clear and smooth. So buckle up!" I was feeling pretty confident in the pilot, but I assure you that the other person in my row and I pulled our seatbelts plenty tight.

Just as predicted—*bam!*—we hit the worst turbulence I had ever flown through. It felt like we were in a toy airplane and some kid was playing with it. The plane would shake violently, dip left, and then abruptly veer to the right. It would be calm for just a moment, then the intensity would increase again. Even I, the frequent flier, was starting to wonder about our safety, not to mention the captain's sanity for flying into that air. After about ten minutes, the pilot came back on and said, "Sorry folks, it's going to last another five minutes or so. Again, all is well!" I am not a nervous flier, but on this trip I was starting to feel a bit nervous. The captain's message, though, helped to keep me calm.

All leaders should understand why the pilot's announcement had such power: It was action-oriented. He did several things:

- He did not underestimate the turbulence.

- He clearly and plainly articulated the plan of action.

- He let us know what his expectations were.

- He let us know what we should expect.

Then he did what made the whole experience fascinating to me:

- He modeled certainty.

While those 15 minutes were by no means pleasant, the captain modeled certainty in everything he did, which created a group of passengers who were, for the most part, calm and confident. While there are times when getting ready creates certainty, there are many other times when getting too ready breeds insecurity in your followers. Imagine if the pilot had spent an hour flying around in circles before entering the turbulence, telling the passengers that he was "getting ready" to fly through it. How confident would we have felt then? Not very! Instead, by taking action and driving forward, you, like the airline captain, can demonstrate the kind of courage and fortitude that emboldens your followers. In addition, driving your direct reports into action and encouraging involvement and initiative is critical to building high performance.

> Driving your direct reports into action and encouraging involvement and initiative is critical to building high performance.

Before you close this chapter and run back to work yelling, "*Charge!*," it will be useful for you to explore what you must manifest in order to drive action in your followers. More importantly, you need to know what you must avoid.

You must manifest leadership that has a certain amount of tolerance for imperfection and risk, and most importantly, a non-punitive style of dealing with mistakes (unless, of course, those mistakes must be dealt with more harshly, such as criminal activity, followers' safety, etc.). Most of the time when leaders create trouble, it's because their words and behavior don't sync up. They say they want action, courage, and innovation, but every time someone sticks his or her neck out, it gets whacked. If you are going to build a culture in which people take action and aren't afraid to boldly step out, then you had better be courageous enough to endure a lack of perfection and a dab of chaos. While action-oriented people who produce outstanding results can do so within the boundaries established by their organizations, they are always pushing those limits.

Don't send them *out there* unless you are *out there* first.

I am encouraging you to drive action sooner rather than later—to create an organization that increases efficiency and action by infusing urgency into your tasks. The most courageous way to do that is to model it—to get in front of your followers and do what my pilot did in the turbulence. Don't send them *out there* unless you are *out there* first. If you want to demonstrate cowardly leadership, encourage action *out there* while you play it safe *in here*. Not only can your employees sense overcaution and overplanning, but so can your competition, and they will not hesitate to take advantage of it. In Chapter 10, we talked about balance and blending logic with intuition. Here again, it is important to balance the *getting ready* with the *getting busy*. I encourage you to err on the side of getting busy.

It is important to balance the *getting ready* with the *getting busy*.

Here are four steps to help you get started:

1. Build an outline of each project plan. Make the end result very clear.

2. Establish who is accountable for each part of the project. This will help followers know where to start.

3. Lead from the front by modeling action. When you start, they will start.

4. Encourage action and reward *anything* that comes close to getting busy instead of getting ready.

———

For a download of a worksheet for this chapter and others please go to www.leadershipisntforcowards.com or scan the QR code.

Leadership Isn't for
Cowards Workbook

CHAPTER 12

How Present Are You?

Section 3 has been all about taking action. We started with the balance between your facts and your gut, then we evaluated the idea of readiness, taking action, and how to motivate your followers to move forward as well. In this chapter, we turn the light more brightly on you.

Most leaders are so busy thinking about what their followers are doing that they don't consider their own mindfulness and preparation. You, however, are already about a third of the way through this book, so congratulations! You are actually doing something to prepare yourself for the demands your leadership places on you. This chapter will deal with your moment-to-moment work as a leader.

> Most leaders are so busy thinking about what their followers are doing that they don't consider their own mindfulness and preparation.

Life is fleeting and opportunities are fragile, and yet sometimes we forget that. There is a tendency to focus on what was or what is to come. We have an almost obsessive need to reflect on our past or consider our future while ignoring the present.

All we have is right this minute. In this minute, there is every opportunity to fully live, to fully engage, and to fully lead and influence those in your care. When you forsake the present in favor of the future or the past, you deny the opportunity to lead right here, right now. It takes courage to be fully present. It takes discipline to not look at your phone, check your email, or think about tomorrow's agenda when a person under your influence is talking to you.

I am not suggesting that you should not plan for the future. I am not suggesting that you ignore the past instead of learning from it.

What I am suggesting is that all the planning and reflecting in the world provide no guarantees. No matter what you do, you can't be certain of the future. You are, however, guaranteed this current moment, by virtue of the fact that you are living it. If you decide to trade this moment for the memory of yesterday or the concern of tomorrow, you are likely to miss what's happening now. Worry, anticipation, regret, and hope are some of the mental processes that rob us of fully and courageously experiencing our leadership and influence on a day-to-day basis.

I can almost hear you saying, "Hold it, hold it, hold it! Did you just say that hope can rob us of fully leading right now?" Yes, that is exactly what I said. If you keep hoping things will get better—hoping a weak follower will start performing, hoping that a plan will eventually be executed, hoping that the market will shift—you will trade your current influence over those things for the anticipation of tomorrow. Instead of boldly taking action, as we discussed in the last chapter, you continue to wait. There is simply no time to waste on that.

How well are you prepared, mentally and emotionally, to lead courageously when hesitation and caution are the norm? Take a moment to think about that. When have you recently stepped out and taken action to impact the present moment?

I urge you to consider how your leadership might be different if you decided, for just a few days, to go ahead and plan for tomorrow, but once it was planned, return to the moment and commit 100 percent of your energy to *now*. What kind of results could you produce in the moment? What kind of relationships could you create if your energy was fully invested? What kind of stress could you eliminate if you stopped worrying about the next day or the next quarter? How often do you rush down the hall to the next meeting or try to get ahead on tomorrow's work instead of seeing what impact you can have today?

The most power you possess as a leader is right here, right now, in this moment. If you prefer the artistic elements of leadership, do not get lost in a whimsical sense of the future. Bolt yourself to the facts in the moment and filter those facts through your gut. For those of you who prefer the scientific approach to leadership and perhaps feel that this chapter is a bit warm and fuzzy for you, I encourage you to think of times when you have targeted your time and energy like a laser. How much more powerful would your leadership be if you focused your energy in the now, sensing what is happening? Think of followers who are stuck and imagine what could happen to their performance if you helped them, too, focus their energy on the present. Encouraging them to deal with what is right in front of them will have significant positive impact on their results.

With all of the swirling information and competing priorities being thrown at you every day, not only from the media but from friends and family and all manner of opinion sources, it is critical that *you* think. Too often in life and business, we don't really think for ourselves. Now, before you dismiss me as stating the obvious, let's think about it. Do you really take the time every week to think about what you are doing? Do you take the time to ask yourself the kind of questions that require you to form opinions from scratch? Are you challenging yourself to be fully awake in your choices and behaviors or are you relying on secondhand impressions? More times than not, great leaders help their followers *think* differently. They encourage, even demand, that their reports consider different perspectives and think for themselves, and they model that behavior in their own lives. It takes very little adjustment in your thinking and your followers' thinking before huge shifts in performance start to take place. It starts with you and how present you are in your work.

> Great leaders help their followers *think* differently.

Some years ago, our firm was asked by our largest client at the time to assist in a search for a new CEO. The request came from their current CEO, for whom I have immense respect. He had decided to retire and, as hard as I worked to talk him out of it, his mind was made up. Our firm doesn't usually do executive search work, but because of our relationship, we agreed to manage the search.

One day, the CEO and I were in his office, he at his desk and me across from him. I pointed at the chair he was sitting in and commented, "I have no idea how we will fill that chair. Your legacy and success here are significant!"

I will never forget what happened next. He said, "Mike, that's not what you were hired to do. You are not being asked to fill this chair.

Come with me." He had a patio off of his office. On that patio was a chair. He pointed at the chair and said, "That is the chair you are being asked to fill."

I was admittedly confused and told him I didn't understand. He said, "The chair at my desk is easy to fill. Honestly, anyone can do it. That is the chair where I review financials, meet with VPs, and make all kinds of business decisions." Pointing back at the chair on his patio, he said, "This is the chair where I sit to think about the future of this company and how I can take steps in the present toward that future. It's the place where I crafted my initial vision for the company. It's the place where I sit and think! Your job is to find a person that can sit here."

That is the point of this chapter. For the CEO to leave his desk and move to the patio was not only a physical move but a metaphorical one as well. To step away and take the time to think, he had to be present in the moment and present in his role as leader. Are you prepared for that seat? Do you afford yourself the opportunity to think, or do the duties of the desk shackle you? Do you take advantage of each moment of each day? Your presence as a leader relates to the heart and soul of who you are much more than it does to what you do, and if you commit to being both thoughtful and present, your leadership and vision will become much more effective and much easier to enact.

> Your presence as a leader relates to the heart and soul of who you are much more than it does to what you do.

Here are four things you can do:

1. Take time once a week to get to the "patio chair" and think about your organization. What vision do you have for its future? What can you do today to move toward that vision?

2. Commit to being fully present, without distraction, for at least one day a week. That means no rushing, no overanalyzing yesterday, and only minimal conversation about tomorrow. Stay with the now.

3. Invite someone (your assistant, a trusted friend) to hold you accountable for being in the moment and indulging in time spent in thought.

4. Channel your energy into things you can control. If you try to create certainty for tomorrow, you'll sacrifice what you could be doing today.

For a download of a worksheet for this chapter and others please go to www.leadershipisntforcowards.com or scan the QR code.

Leadership Isn't for
Cowards Workbook

CHAPTER 13

Do You Remember a Time when You Hesitated and Lost?

Act or be lost in the back of the pack. This entire section points to the simple truth that action is usually the key to solving problems, achieving goals, and enjoying the most success. It

> **Act or be lost in the back of the pack.**

is interesting that when we hear other people explain their failures to achieve goals or to meet expectations, we think they're making *excuses*, but when we explain our own failures, we're giving *reasons*. Can we just take a minute here to admit that most of the reasons why we don't succeed are because we didn't do something? That most of our *reasons* are actually *excuses?* In our litigious, lawsuit-heavy climate, everyone seems to have become more hesitant. When did we begin to soften so much? When did we become so comfortable making excuses for our failure to act?

As I write this, the U.S. economy is full of uncertainty and the electorate's palpable frustration with the federal government is at an all-time high. Ask the average person on the street and they will tell you that the bulk of their frustration is due to politicians' failure to act and get engaged with the nation's problems. When blame is the primary strategic tool, as in much of politics, failure is the likely result. It's no different in business. When time and energy is wasted on excuse-making and hesitation, you and your team will feel the drain. Do not hesitate. Do not tolerate hesitation. Decide, then act.

To what extent is your leadership style action-oriented? If you consider yourself a take-charge, action-oriented leader, the rest of your team should reflect this. Do your direct reports know—really know—that hesitation is only an option if danger is apparent, but that in all other cases, they are expected to act? In this chapter, we will explore things that hold you back from taking action.

There will, of course, be those who want to resist action by saying that sometimes hesitation is good—sometimes it is necessary. Of course, that is true . . . sometimes. In the example you're thinking of right now, it's probably not the case. I would venture to say that hesitation and resistance to action do far more damage and destroy far more opportunities than mistaken action ever could. If that is true, then why is it so difficult to act? There is one main reason: fear.

> **Hesitation and resistance to action do far more damage and destroy far more opportunities than mistaken action ever could.**

If there is fear in your organization, people will not act. They can have the best intentions, but if pain is the result of taking action, then your direct reports will go miles out of their way to avoid doing so. Remember, it is human instinct to avoid pain. However, what you think of as painful may not always be so.

Not long ago, I made a post to my Facebook page encouraging leaders to act boldly. Someone responded to the post by saying, "What if you work for an organization that talks the talk, but if you act on what they say, you get your wings clipped and are passively told to go back to your desk and not make waves?" I am sure that his generalization was true, through a narrow point of view. However, there is a natural tendency we all have to ignore information that contradicts or does not support our beliefs about the world, especially our negative beliefs (earlier in the book, we talked about that tendency as bias). If we believe someone doesn't like us, we will see only those behaviors that support that impression. If we think we are bad at something, we will see only more evidence of that conclusion. As one of my favorite philosophers, Julia Roberts, said in the movie *Pretty Woman*, "The bad things are easier to believe."

In fact, this tendency to see only information that agrees with our beliefs is so strong that it will often blind us to contrary evidence. As long as we don't see other possibilities, we don't have to take action. If you really believe you will get your hand slapped if you take any action at all, and worse, if your hand has been slapped for doing so, then fear will stop you from trying again and your natural tendencies will stop you from seeing evidence that it might be different next time.

It takes courage to act in the face of fear. In fact, it is only when fear and risk are present that people need courage. If you suspect pain might follow action, you must be courageous to step out anyway.

Remember, it is unlikely that *every* action you take will result in pain, but if you submit to fear in one area, it's likely to affect other areas of your life. If I were able to talk directly with the guy that posted on my Facebook, I would ask him if it was 100 percent true that action was punished in his workplace. Were people who came up with new ideas punished? Were people who expressed opinions punished? Were employees who came up with cheaper ways to do things or ways to increase efficiency punished? Probably not.

I have never seen an organization that punishes all action. Believing that is simply an excuse. Fear is the real problem, and it seems bigger the more you dwell on it. Think of kids who say nobody at school likes them, when the truth is that one kid said something mean to them one day. Extinguish as much fear as possible in your life, and then action will be easier to take.

> Fear is the real problem, and it seems bigger the more you dwell on it.

So, what is fear? Simply put, fear is a negative prediction about the future. Keep in mind that people are never afraid of something itself, they are afraid of the result of the thing: They are not afraid of flying; they are afraid of crashing. They are not afraid of speaking in public; they are afraid of being judged or disliked. They are not afraid of snakes; they are afraid of being bitten. Therefore, people are not afraid of taking action; they are afraid of what will happen if they take action.

> People are not afraid of taking action; they are afraid of what will happen if they take action.

Whether or not you take action is governed by a simple ratio: your perception of danger versus your confidence in your ability to cope. If you know you can handle whatever comes your way, the amount of fear you feel is minimized and you will step out. If you perceive greater danger than your confidence can handle, you won't. (You'll notice it's your *perception* of danger, not necessarily the actual danger. If you can evaluate the real danger, as opposed to the perceived danger, your picture of the situation becomes more rational and you will be more motivated to act.) When your followers are stopped by fear, the easy thing to do is to tell them to act anyway, but if that seems to have diminishing returns, you can quickly trigger action by managing their fear–confidence ratio. Here's a six-question exercise to help you do that:

1. What's the worst thing that could happen?

    This is not a rhetorical question. Really examine the worst case scenario. Always start with this because the brain emphasizes the worst possibilities the most, so you need to get it out of the way.

2. What's the best thing that could happen?

3. What's the most likely thing that will happen?

    Then, consider these:

4. What's my specific plan if the worst thing happens?

    This exercise will fail if this question is answered with a cliché, such as, "Oh, we'll just cross that bridge when we come to it." If the bridge is washed out when you come to it, you will be out of options. Remember, action is easier when coping mechanisms are clear.

5. What's my specific plan if the best thing happens?

6. What's my specific plan if the most likely thing happens?

Answering these questions will help you clear away fear-causing doubt and uncertainty and make it much easier to motivate yourself and others into action.

Four things to do:

1. Insist that action be rewarded and mistakes be tolerated.

2. Be clear about where the boundaries are for action and mistakes. Vague rules make action more intimidating, so be sure everyone knows your guidelines.

3. Publicly and loudly acknowledge people who take action.

4. Use the six-question exercise to reduce fear and hesitation.

For a download of a worksheet for this chapter and others please go to www.leadershipisntforcowards.com or scan the QR code.

Leadership Isn't for
Cowards Workbook

CHAPTER 14

Are You In, or Aren't You?

Have you ever received a gift from a friend, family member, or other such generous person and realized upon opening it that you just didn't like it? Years ago I received a Christmas present from my girlfriend at the time. It was . . . special. She made me wait to open it last. She told me it was her favorite gift and the one she was most excited about giving me. It was wrapped nicely, about the size of a piece of paper, and I had no idea what it was. I eagerly unwrapped it and realized that it was a gift certificate—and not just any gift certificate. It said, "You are hereby entitled to one free sky-diving adventure!"

I remember looking at her and thinking, did I ask to jump out of a plane for Christmas? She said, "Isn't it great? Aren't you excited?" I was not really all that fired up about the idea, but when I expressed my lack of enthusiasm she said, "Come on! I've jumped out of a plane twice, and I'm a girl! You aren't going to let a girl outdo you, are you?"

"Um, yes, actually," I thought. "I think I'm cool with that!" She gave enough, well, encouragment, until finally I agreed. I don't think there is a better illustration of taking action than what I experienced on that adventure.

When we arrived at the skydiving airport about two hours from my home, I was escorted into a room where I was shown a video of a lawyer. He shared with me that what I was about to do was very dangerous and that they had no insurance—zero, zip, nada. In order to jump, I had to release any and all liability by signing a small mountain of paperwork they placed in front of me. "Nice," I thought. "I may die and there's nothing that can be done about it. That's always the best way to start an experience."

I was then escorted to a room where other adventurists sat waiting to be instructed on the best practices for leaping out of a perfectly good airplane. In came the chief instructor, who gave us very detailed instructions about how to survive and enjoy a jump from 12,000 feet. He told us that we would be introduced to our instructors. Then we would get on a plane and climb to 12,000 feet. At the appropriate time, we would walk to the back of the airplane, hook up to our instructors, and, when directed to do so, we would rock three times and gently roll out of the airplane. "Right," I thought. "Just gently roll out of the plane." Immediately upon jumping, the instructor would tap us on the shoulders, indicating it was time to spread our arms and legs. When we got down to 5,000 feet, our instructors would tap us twice on the right hip. This was our cue to pull the orange rip cords attached to our jump suits that would, in turn, open our parachutes.

After this quick lesson in skydiving, we were escorted to a garage-like room where we were equipped with jump suits (very tight), altimeters (devices that tell you your altitude), and goggles. I hired a videographer to tape my demise and out we went to watch another group jump.

As we stood looking skyward, I asked the instructor what we were watching. He said we were waiting for that teeny, tiny spec in the sky (apparently an airplane) to fly over so the people could jump and we could watch. Right on cue, tiny little human dots started coming out of the bigger dot. Seconds later, parachutes starting opening.

All except one. I looked at the instructor and said, "Uh, this isn't what the brochure promised!"

He said, "That guy is crazy. He jumps here all the time and he's a competitive jumper." Seconds passed. Parachute still not open. I started to get worried. Then, finally, at what seemed like the last second, the chute spread out above the jumper's head.

As the group landed, they walked over to us. The crazy guy with the late parachute walked right up to me. "Is your name Mike Staver?"

I got a sick feeling in my stomach and said, "Nope."

He said, "Yes it is. I'm your instructor." This was the man who was going to be strapped to my back and tell me when to pull the cord to open my parachute to make sure I didn't die. Wonderful.

We got on the plane and hooked ourselves up to our instructors, and as the plane reached 12,000 feet, we lined up to exit the nice, safe airplane. My crazy instructor and I were third in line. The first pair jumped with no worries. As the second pair, a female instructor and a female student, got to the door, the student started screaming, "I've changed my mind! I've changed mind! I've changed my mind!"

"Too late!" her instructor yelled. Out they went.

Now it was my turn. My instructor asks, "Do you want to do the regular jump, or do you want to have some fun?"

"Uhh . . ." I'm on video, so what am I supposed to say? "Of course I want to have some fun." Remember now, we were supposed to rock three times and gently roll out of the airplane. Well, apparently, "having some fun" did not include "gently rolling out of the airplane." He yelled, "Let's go!" With that, he did three huge, abrupt rocks, spun us around backward, and out we went, plummeting through the air with nothing beneath us but the ground. As we left the plane, we did a backflip and three somersaults. You know that feeling that you have when you are on a roller coaster or go over a hill in the car—the feeling of butterflies in your stomach, like you're falling? When you jump out of an airplane, you feel that same feeling, but only for a second. Then you have the sensation of flying. It's an exhilarating experience. We flew from 12,000 feet to 5,000 feet in seconds. I later learned that we were going almost 100 mph. Talk about wind in your face! What a rush! I highly recommend it.

You may be thinking, what does that have to do with action? It has everything to do with it! It all comes down to the differences between the jump of the woman in front of me and my own jump. These two examples are illustrations of how you can approach action.

In her case, she was prepared, she was safe, and she had an experienced mentor, and yet when it came to the moment of truth, she didn't want to do it. As we discussed in the last chapter, her perception of danger was high and she wasn't particularly confident that the plan she had was enough to protect her. The instructor basically said, "Your fear is irrelevant to me. You are going, and I am going with you," and forced her out of the plane. She required external action to drive her behavior.

In my case, I too was prepared, had my safety gear and had an experienced, if a bit crazy, mentor. If I didn't trust myself, I trusted him. In fact, my instructor (read: leader) asked me if I wanted to take it up a notch. He assessed whether or not I was willing to increase my performance. While I'm not sure if the flips and turns increased the danger, I am very certain that they increased the intensity of the experience! They required different choices and different behaviors than a regular jump, but they enhanced it and made it better. All it took was my willingness to try. Where the woman who went before me required external action to motivate her, I used a process of internal action to drive my performance to new levels.

The difference between internal action and external action is the foundation for high performance and success. You as the leader must assess which type of action your direct reports need in order to perform at the highest levels. Do you need to encourage them to achieve, or do you just need to ask them, "How much better do you want to be?" and let their own decisions do the rest? You may have a follower who needs to learn to give better presentations to advance his career, yet his fear of public speaking has prevented him from taking that next step. That would require your external action to direct him to take a presentation skills class. You may have a customer service rep who is hesitant in making decisions to satisfy customers, for fear of making the wrong decision. You would need to tell her to take risks while reassuring her that she won't be punished. Alternatively, you may have a direct report who is highly motivated, but a bit confused, and just needs to be pointed in the right direction.

My bias is that if your followers don't eventually learn to be motivated by internal action, then they will be compliant with expectations while never fully committing and engaging. They will adopt a wait-for-direction mindset rather than a take-initiative mindset, and it will be hard to prompt them to take action in anything.

Internal action has to do with resolve, choice, determination, commitment, surrender, and learning, while external action requires the simple physical achievement of tasks. If you are asked to do something by your boss that you don't really want to do or that you think is a waste of time, you may do it, but internally you will not be committed. Your external actions align with the request, but your internal action does not. External action without internal action usually appears as the result of a request, expectation, or demand from some external source. The highest level of performance requires both external and internal action to be in alignment. While the woman who jumped out in front of me got the job done, I am not certain she enjoyed it.

It is not always necessary that you or your direct reports take internal action. Sometimes you just have to do what you have to do. But if you want to create a high-performance organization, if you want to be the head of a group that consistently wins, then you need both. If you can force external action but not overcome internal resistance, you will feel like you are pulling a car through the mud to get things done.

This is the last chapter in this section. We have spent quite a few pages making the case for action. There is no doubt that action drive results. A plan doesn't drive results, willpower doesn't drive results, and not even goals drive results. Action drives results. Period. So get out there and act.

> A plan doesn't drive results, willpower doesn't drive results, and not even goals drive results. Action drives results. Period.

Here are five ways to get started:

1. If you don't know what to do first, find a model or guide and do what they do.

2. Drive action even when you don't feel completely sure by encouraging small steps. You can always backtrack later.

3. Be clear about the internal and external action you need from yourself first and your people second.

4. Constantly ask questions. (What needs to happen for this to be completed on time? What is keeping us from winning this sale? How much support do you need from me to make this successful?) Be observant about whether your followers are motivated by internal or external action, or both.

5. Point out and eliminate activities that slow progress.
    Remember, action is often as much about what you stop doing
    as it is about what you start doing.

    ───────────────

For a download of a worksheet for this chapter and others please go to
www.leadershipisntforcowards.com or scan the QR code.

Leadership Isn't for
Cowards Workbook

TAKE RESPONSIBILITY

The second T in ATTACK is for *take responsibility*. You know how important action is to the courageous leader, but action without responsibility can have a negative impact. Organizations that encourage, even demand, personal responsibility are healthier and smarter. In this section, you will learn the differences between blame and responsibility. You will see how to clearly articulate and apply steps to create a culture of followers who take ownership of their responsibility.

CHAPTER 15

Want to Responsibly Scare Some People?

A m I the only one who wonders if we live in a world where fewer and fewer people want to take responsibility for themselves and their behavior? Have you noticed how many people just want to blame someone else? It seems that people spend so much time finger-pointing that they really don't take the time to consider how they may have contributed to their own circumstances.

I was walking behind a couple with a stroller in a mall one day (some people call it stalking) and I noticed that on the seat of the stroller there was a label in print large enough to read from ten feet away; it said, "Warning." I thought, "How nice of them to warn us about the little hellion in the stroller!"

When they stopped, I walked up to them and asked why they had left the warning label attached. They said they had just purchased the stroller but might leave the label on because it was so funny. I asked, "Why is it funny?"

They said, "Read the fine print." I got closer. The small letters said, "Do not fold stroller with baby in seat."

Seriously? Should you really be reproducing if you need that warning? Why is that label necessary? Why does that cardboard shade thing you can put in your windshield in the summer say, "Remove before driving"? Why does the car lift at the repair garage say, "Do not stand under lift when lowering car"? Why does a coffee cup say, "Caution! The beverage you are about to enjoy is extremely hot"? (Perhaps it would be more helpful if it said, "Caution! You just paid $5 for a cup of coffee! This could lead to further irrational purchases!")

Of course, the reason all of those items have those warnings on them is because somebody sued somebody else or somebody is preemptively avoiding being sued. Companies are afraid that consumers will not take responsibility for accidents that happen while using their products.

A courageous leader promotes personal responsibility in the organization.

At some point, courageous and healthy people take responsibility for their contributions to their failures and more readily share the credit for their successes. A courageous leader promotes personal responsibility in the organization on a regular basis. The process of infusing that responsibility into your organization begins with you. To what extent do you take responsibility for your own contributions, both positive and negative? To what extent do your direct reports know that if you have participated in the failure of a project, you are going to own it immediately? To what extent do they know that your head will explode if you hear them whining, blaming, and making excuses?

To create a courageous organization, it is critical that you make personal responsibility a part of it. I am reminded of a financial institution's branch vice president who creatively explained or deflected every problem his followers reported about him. He had absolute, unyielding resistance against the idea that he might have contributed to his employees' unhappiness. Eventually, he was able to accept responsibility, and his growth as a leader could move forward, but it wasn't easy.

It's not supposed to be easy. A good old-fashioned dose of humility, mixed with some ownership of faults and changes in behavior, is a challenge. It is supposed to be challenging. If you are reading this and believe taking responsibility is easy for you, I respectfully suggest that you aren't paying close enough attention to your faults. It takes courage and a strong sense of self to stare in the mirror and accept that the person looking back at you participated in, and even directly caused, something unpleasant and undesirable. However, the ability to do so is absolutely necessary. It is through taking responsibility that you make your leadership the most powerful.

Why bother, though? If you're a leader and you have power, then why not just cast responsibility off onto the market, the people you can't count on, an inferior product, the people in the corporate office, and so on? Why not try to avoid consequences? The simple answer is if you avoid responsibility, responsibility will eventually come back to get you.

> **If you avoid responsibility, responsibility will eventually come back to get you.**

One night, I was flipping through TV channels, not really paying much attention, when I came across one of those old movies. I don't know what made me stop to watch it, but I did. It was titled *The Caine Mutiny*. I had never had an interest in the movie and I didn't even know what it was about, but that night I decided to see if I liked it.

In the movie, Lt. Cmdr. Philip Francis Queeg (played by Humphrey Bogart) is overthrown during a typhoon and loses command of his ship. The mutineers are put on trial. Toward the end of the movie, Commander Queeg is on the witness stand being questioned by the mutineers' defense attorney in order to prove that the overthrow was just and right. As the attorney asks question after question about Queeg's questionable behavior and outbursts of anger, almost every answer is the same: Queeg blames a disloyal crew for all of the problems he had. Were it not for them, he ranted, he wouldn't have had to do the things he did to solve problems.

In the movie, they were trying to prove that Queeg was crazy, so that's where the analogy breaks down, but my point stands. There are many times when the only answer people give is, "It's everyone else's fault," and while they sit there throwing blame around, things continue to get worse. I am not sure how much more fear-driven a leader can be than to blame people, places, things, and events for the challenges faced. It's the opposite of what you should be doing.

Want to really scare some people? Stand up in front of your direct reports and own up to something you did that you shouldn't have, or something you didn't do that you should have. Want to build loyalty? Own your mistakes. Want to settle a fight with your significant other? Say, "I have been thinking about the disagreement we had, and I want you to know that I admit my part in it. I realized that my behavior contributed to the tension and frustration, and I am sorry. Here is what I'm going to do differently."

When I use that example, people often say to me, "Mike, people don't talk that way." I generally respond, "I know. That's why I have a job!" People may not talk that way, but they should.

Take those suggested sentences and break them down. They have the necessary elements of courageousness and can be formatted the same way again and again. First, you have an excuse-free, unqualified acknowledgment of responsibility. There were no *buts* in the sentence; it wasn't, "I own my part, *but* you have to own your part, too!"

Next there is an apology. Say you're sorry for any harm you caused.

> Apologies are worthless unless there is associated behavior change.

Finally, there is a commitment to change your behavior. Apologies are worthless unless there is associated behavior change to make sure the offense doesn't happen again. So many times, people will say they are sorry as if it's a "get out of a difficult conversation free" card. Let's be clear—accepting responsibility is only the start of the journey. Changing behavior is where the real power comes out. It's one thing to accept your participation in a problem. It's another to commit to a shift in your behavior. The most effective way to take responsibility is to own it, apologize for it, commit to the change, and then actually change your behavior.

Of all of the things we have covered so far, I don't think any other area of leadership requires more courage than taking responsibility. I also don't think there is another one that will garner more respect. Bringing the idea of self-responsibility into your organization requires courage as well. It takes a courageous leader to ask the tough questions and require people to stand up and own their parts in the challenges facing your group. It also takes discipline and strength to endure discomfort. In the end, though, it will be worth it. The following chapters will help you create an organization of highly accountable people, but for now, here are five ways to get started:

1. Evaluate how much personal responsibility is being acknowledged or not acknowledged in your organization.

2. Speak up about the expectation that people start taking responsibility.

3. Come from a place of humility by asking the tough questions of yourself first. Ask, "How might I have contributed to this problem?"

4. Commit to two or three specific behavior changes to make up for a prior mistake.

5. Practice using all three parts of the phrase we discussed to admit your responsibility to other people.

For a download of a worksheet for this chapter and others please go to www.leadershipisntforcowards.com or scan the QR code.

Leadership Isn't for
Cowards Workbook

CHAPTER 16

How Much Blame Can You Take?

W e know from Chapter 13 that blame cripples your ability to act. Now let's discuss it in more detail.

Blame is the opposite of responsibility. Kids blame their parents, employees blame their bosses, the worst salespeople blame their customers, businesspeople blame the economy, and all it does is shift responsibility to someone else. Blame is an energy-draining, counterproductive way of dealing with difficult circumstances. So while, in

> **Blame is an energy-draining, counterproductive way of dealing with difficult circumstances.**

the last chapter, we talked about accepting your own responsibility and emphasizing responsibility in your organization, we were not talking about blame. Blaming someone else puts you in the position of a victim, like something happened to you outside of your control; therefore, you won't take action to change your circumstances because it's somebody else's problem. Personal responsibility frees you to act because you realize you have the power to create a solution to the problem. Personal responsibility creates opportunity, while blame creates paralysis.

In one of my recent projects, a manager in a company was mad at his boss because the boss wouldn't do things the way he thought the boss should. In fact, he was so locked into blame that he actually believed he was paralyzed to act until his boss changed. His relentless blaming of the boss paralyzed his own leadership. Instead of courageously leading, he continued to wait for his boss to make the first move. When I asked him if he believed he played any part in the problem, he strongly reminded

> **Personal responsibility creates opportunity, while blame creates paralysis.**

me that he couldn't do a single thing until his boss stopped waiting and moved off the dime.

Organizations can be crippled by blame just as much as people. Blame-based companies always look for a person to take the fall when something goes wrong. It is almost as if there will be no peace until they can find someone to blame, even though sometimes no one is at fault, or everybody is collectively responsible. When so much energy is invested in seeking the *bad guy*, vital and scarce resources are drained away from activities that could otherwise create outstanding results. Instead of finding a solution and moving forward, focus is diverted to trying to pin responsibility on someone for things that he or she often have zero control over.

Blame-based leadership seeks to find a bad guy so that there is someone to absorb the problem, like a lightning rod absorbs a bolt of otherwise dangerous electricity. If a bad guy can be found, then everyone else can take a collective sigh of relief. For that particular problem, they think that they are off the hook. If it's marketing's fault, then operations can't possibly be responsible for the train wreck. If it's operations' fault, management can't have done anything wrong. If management messed up, then marketing surely didn't make any mistakes. People think, "As long as it's not my fault, then it's certainly not my responsibility to fix it."

Of course, that's not true. Whether or not you accept responsibility, a problem can still hurt your productivity. The manager of a real estate office was delivering news about a change that was being made to the services offered to the real estate agents. The manager believed that the agents would respond negatively to the changes so she decided to tell them that the corporate office had decided to change the services in question. She mistakenly thought that by making it corporate's fault, she would align herself closer with the agents. Instead, the agents began going around her back to people in the corporate office, thus eroding her credibility and influence. It would have been better had she simply explained the changes and asked for questions. Even though she shifted responsibility elsewhere, the problem still hurt her and her people. Furthermore, the amount of time wasted in finger-pointing and seeking the bad guy is everyone's fault.

If no one stands up and says, "Who cares whose fault it is? Let's get to fixing it and moving forward!" then everyone must take their share of wasted time and energy.

Sit in a sales meeting and listen to people talk about their successes and failures. Good salespeople don't blame their customers, the market, the corporate office, and so on for their failures. The successful salesperson focuses on things over which he or she has control. Blaming the customer means the customer has to change before success can be achieved, and since the salesperson has no direct control over that, he or she will get stuck in failure.

How do you identify blame? Any time you hear a direct report or a colleague say that a problem is someone else's fault or the result of unfairness, you are likely hearing from a person mired deeply in blame. You can't have that mentality in your organization, and change starts with you. Solutions cannot be effectively found unless you as a leader decide enough is enough. Until you publicly put a stake in the ground and tell your people that blame is no longer an acceptable strategy, they will likely continue to use it. And why wouldn't they? It's easier than accepting responsibility, it's less work, it makes you feel better about yourself, and most of the world will let you get away with it.

Avoiding blame means accepting the fact that, while you would like to blame others for the choices *you* have made, you know that *you* alone are responsible for them. Acknowledging that you are ultimately responsible for the results of your life, thoughts, and actions creates a level of freedom not experienced by those who choose to blame others. It empowers you to act. Courageous leaders are driven by, even obsessed with, the imperative to eliminate excuse-making and blame from themselves and their organizations. Your job is simply to acknowledge problems and drive your people to solve them immediately. As long as they are allowed to focus on the things that are out of their control, they will continue to wallow in the ineffectiveness created by blame. That kind

> Courageous leaders are driven by, even obsessed with, the imperative to eliminate excuse-making and blame from themselves and their organizations.

of life-sucking activity will leave your group wandering aimlessly instead of proactively addressing issues as they arise.

When the 2010 Winter Olympics were held in British Columbia, there were some problems with the amount of snow on the slopes. While I'm not a skier, I think I can safely say that snow is a pretty critical element in the Winter Olympics. Though the media seemed to be talking a lot about the conditions, I was impressed by how little the athletes discussed it. As champions, they acknowledged their circumstances and then turned their focus back to themselves and the things they could do to make the best of it. Highly successful athletes, artists, singers, salespeople, leaders, and employees dismiss things outside of their control and focus on the things they can do to have impact. "Who cares about conditions?" they say. "I will shape my own destiny." That attitude marks the kind of leader who will generate memorable and powerful results.

As this chapter draws to a close, let's address the most dangerous kind of blame: blaming and berating yourself for a decision, a failure, a broken promise, or other mistake. I am obviously a big believer in personal responsibility, and I am unyielding in my expectation that mistakes and failures be acknowledged and dealt with. What I am completely against is relentlessly beating yourself up because of those mistakes or failures. Acknowledge your responsibility, apologize to anyone you hurt, and move forward with action steps that will rectify the mistake or help you avoid repeating it as you go forward. Punishing yourself for hours and hours, weeks and weeks, or even years and years will only suck the life and potential out of you. It takes huge energy to hold on to blame. Let it go! Accept what is yours, and move on. Continuing to look back can only lead to poor results.

> It takes huge energy to hold on to blame. Let it go! Accept what is yours, and move on.

Here are three things you can do:

1. When you catch yourself blaming others, stop. Honestly consider what your own part in the problem may have been.

2. Ask your direct reports to do the same thing. When blame starts to arise in a conversation, direct everyone back toward responsibility.

3. If you are beating yourself up for a mistake, let it go. Instead of feeling bad, see what you might do to make it right.

For a download of a worksheet for this chapter and others please go to www.leadershipisntforcowards.com or scan the QR code.

Leadership Isn't for
Cowards Workbook

CHAPTER 17

What Difference Do You Make?

Accepting responsibility and letting go of blame have been the core ideas in this section. These ideas are so integral to courageous leadership that one could write an entire book about them; what will be the impact *you* get to have when you fully and courageously absorb and integrate those two concepts? How can you show your followers what to do?

Waaaaay back at the start of this book we talked about how you need to understand that you are messing with people's lives. You have the power to do a lot of good or a lot of harm. The difference you make is the degree to which you drive these concepts deep into your organization. So here you are, no doubt wondering how exactly a leader does that. How can you exhibit the necessary leadership behaviors so that those who report to you not only understand the concept of accepting responsibility, but also apply it to their performance and realize why they should do so?

The first and most effective way is to model it yourself. That is the biggest difference you can make. There is no type of behavioral influence as effective as modeling, particularly when that modeling comes from a person in a position of authority. What you model is simply the story your behavior tells. If someone didn't know you, didn't understand your intentions, had never heard you talk, didn't know your background, and was dropped into your organization to observe you for a month without being allowed

> There is no type of behavioral influence as effective as modeling, particularly when that modeling comes from a person in a position of authority.

to talk to you, what is the story your behavior would tell? If a video of your daily behavior was shown to a group of fellow leaders from across the country, what story would that video tell?

When the speeches are over, the plan is shared, and the vision is spoken, all that is left is your behavior. It is your behavior that tells the loudest story and has the greatest influence. If you're not sure what story you're modeling, ask some other people to tell you. Ask your direct reports to anonymously write down four words that describe what it's like to work for you. That is the story your behavior is modeling for them.

All courageous leaders have a mantra—a consistent theme that they talk about. "Our employees come first" or, "Every problem is an opportunity," or, "Drivers wanted," or, "The power of one" are all examples of mantras that leaders use. What is your mantra? What is the message that your followers can rally around? Do they feel the passion in your voice when you speak to them about it? The best leaders exhibit behavior that clearly and accurately reflects their mantra. They take responsibility for what they say and how well they live up to it. When there is inconsistency between the story you tell and the story you live, credibility and trust erode quickly; therefore, you must model personal responsibility in order to instill it in your followers. Be the first one to step up and shoulder some part of the problem. Be specific about the part you played in creating it.

> When there is inconsistency between the story you tell and the story you live, credibility and trust erode quickly.

I am reminded of the president of a small company who struggled mightily with this idea. While working with him, I drew a pie chart titled "Missed Profit Goal." When I asked him to divide the chart to show who was responsible for the missed target, he was able to divide the chart up into variously-sized pieces and was very compelling in his description of how each of the people and departments in the pie had played a part in the mistake. When he was finished, the pie was completely filled in. Just about the only person missing from it was him. He was unwilling to see the part he played. When I asked him a direct question about his particular role, he was defensive. He found plenty of reasons for the miss, but none of them involved him. He could have said something as simple as, "I didn't ask enough tough questions early on," or, "I allowed my optimism to carry me too far."

Instead of taking ownership, this president blamed other people, and his behavior encouraged his followers to do the same.

On the other extreme, a director was asked about her department's lower-than-expected employee satisfaction scores in a year-end review. Her response to the question was just as poor a model for taking responsibility: "I obviously don't understand my employees and what is going on with them. I am not sure how I could have been so blind to their frustrations and concerns. I really believed I knew what was happening! It's my fault." Unless that is completely true, which is unlikely, she erred on the side of overburdening herself with blame. She could have said a simple, "Clearly, there are challenges with my staff that I have missed! Here is my plan to address those things." Instead she succumbed to beating herself up about it, which will allow her followers to copy the same behavior.

In another failed attempt at taking responsibility, a manager in a manufacturing company was asked to spend time talking with me because someone had taken a complaint about him to human resources. The employee said that the manager would ask for feedback and encourage open, honest communication, but would say things like, "I know I am not a perfect leader, *but* the point I am here to make is that you people need to make changes and make them now." When I talked with this leader, he insisted that he did take responsibility. In reality, he didn't.

There are two problems with his statement to his followers. First, it doesn't admit a specific behavior. Second, the word *but* is always a problem and will always get you into trouble. In this case, the followers probably only heard, "*You* people need to make changes and make them now." The first half of the sentence didn't carry any weight.

The moral of the story is that you need to be specific, be sincere, and avoid over-explanation and *buts*. Too often, leaders will take responsibility but then spend ridiculous amounts of time explaining why they did or didn't do what they did or didn't do. This type of explanation destroys any attempt to take responsibility and wastes everybody's time.

It can be a particular problem when you are talking to your boss. When talking to your boss, make sure that your responsibility ownership is matched with a clear and compelling plan for recovery. Remember, the key is not to fixate on who is responsible and why, but rather to own it, present a solution, and move on. The core of the process is to state your level of responsibility and what you are going to change. Your ability to be clear and concise will create a model that your followers can easily emulate.

> The key is not to fixate on who is responsible and why, but rather to own it, present a solution, and move on.

The challenge, of course, is that they won't just do it because you do it. Modeling the appropriate behavior only sets the stage for your followers and shows them what you expect. It would be nice if they would observe you and say, "Hey, look what our boss is doing! That is great! You know what? I am going to do that, too!" Unfortunately, unless you have very obnoxious kiss-ups for followers (in which case you have other problems), that will never happen. In the next chapter, we will talk about what strategies you can use to get your followers to own their responsibility in three different areas. In the meantime, here are five ideas to help you balance your own responsibility:

1. Whenever there is a challenge in your area of influence, clearly state your role in causing it.

2. Identify specific changes you are going to make to avoid the challenge in the future.

3. Avoid emotional outbursts and beating yourself up.

4. Keep *buts* out of the conversation.

5. Don't waste time on long explanations.

For a download of a worksheet for this chapter and others please go to www.leadershipisntforcowards.com or scan the QR code.

Leadership Isn't for
Cowards Workbook

CHAPTER 18

What Kinds of Responsibility Are You Taking?

Let's face it; you have those times when you look across the conference-room landscape at your followers and think, "Didn't we already have this conversation? I thought I was clear about my expectations! Can't we just solve the problem and move on?" If we are being honest, then we must acknowledge that there are times when we really don't know what we are doing. We have great intentions, great plans, and then—*Bam!*—the execution is lousy. Or we have great intentions, but no plan and no execution whatsoever. When you ask questions about the lack of execution—Why so slow? What happened to the original goal? What is the problem?—there are probably times when you get back some kind of nondescript noise that sounds like Charlie Brown's teacher. Sometimes, you just don't know what to do to get things done.

If you are very fortunate, you have a perfect team that owns its mistakes, changes direction, and then accomplishes results. For the rest of you, this chapter is written to assist you in getting your followers to take responsibility. As we have previously discussed, responsibility is not about looking for the bad guy or seeking to make anyone feel bad. However, it's also not about being so worried about upsetting our followers that we don't ask the tough questions.

I have been fortunate enough to hear many leaders talk to their followers. The best ones are tough without diminishing anyone's self-esteem or self-respect. It is important that your followers leave an interaction with you with the full knowledge that you are on their side and want them to win, first as people, then as your followers. There should

> Leadership is influencing others to achieve results beyond those that they believe are possible.

be no doubt in their minds that you expect the highest degree of execution and performance. The best thing you can do for your followers is to not allow them to settle. Remember, leadership is influencing others to achieve results beyond those that they believe are possible.

One of the first steps in that process is getting them to understand three key areas in which they possess responsibility: their choices, their attitudes/mindsets, and their performance, in that order. As simple as that may look in writing, it is very different in the real world. You want your followers to own the fact that they have choices, that their mindsets drive everything, and their performance is a reflection of those choices and mindsets. If you can do that, then you really do know what you are doing and you will help move your organization toward a culture of responsibility. These three areas will help your followers responsibly solve most challenges they will face. Let's explore them in more detail one by one.

CHOICES

Walk down the cereal aisle of your grocery store and you will realize just how far we have pushed the idea of choice. Look at the book-sized menus of some restaurants and you will see how big a deal choice is to us. But if you're like most people, there comes a point where you have so many choices, it just gets overwhelming. Too many or too few choices can make it hard to know how to choose correctly.

Here's the deal for your followers: They and they alone are responsible for the choices they make. Your job is to talk about that, to blog about it, and to help them understand that we all have choices, and that those choices are solely the responsibility of the chooser. When they come to you with a challenge or concern, ask them what they believe their choices are. Challenge them to consider carefully the full range of choices they have available to them. Do not allow them to negate or avoid the consideration of choices that seem impractical or illogical at first glance. Make certain that they understand that as long as they are alive, they have choices. Never, ever, ever let them say or believe for even a second that they have no choice in something. Coach them to consider the intended and unintended consequences of their choices. Ask them what else they think could happen if they make the decision they are considering. Challenge them to clearly think through their decisions and to pause to reflect. This is particularly important when making very important decisions. Often when making choices, people only consider the outcomes they intend without careful consideration of possible unintended side effects. Ask them to walk you through their thought processes and how they believe the choices they are considering will impact the goals and outcomes they are charged with achieving.

ATTITUDES AND MINDSETS

Attitudes and mindsets are critical. To what extent are you driving, encouraging, and requiring your followers to improve their mindsets all the time? How much of your followers' performance reviews are focused on their attitudes and the behaviors those attitudes create? Clearly explaining your expectations and reasoning, and working with your followers to create the attitudes and mindsets necessary for success, is very important.

As an example, a leader stands up before his followers and says, "It is important that each of us adopts and applies a can-do attitude!" While a can-do attitude is certainly an example of a mindset you want in an organization, it would be more helpful to those listening if there was an associated example of behavior that went with it. For instance, the leader could say, "It is important that each of us adopts and applies a can-do attitude! So going forward, I want to hear more about solutions and less about problems. There needs to be a complete focus on what we *can* do rather on what we *can't* do. I want fewer reasons why we can't and more suggestions for how we can."

Those messages to the group as a whole will make your conversations with individuals easier because they will already know your expectations. Ask your followers questions like: What would you have to believe in order to solve this problem? What other ideas do you have for being able to be more effective? What have you done in the past to deal with problems like this? When you are faced with challenges like this, what is your strategy for working it out? If I wasn't here to talk about this and you had to make a decision alone, what decision would you make?

> Attitudes always manifest themselves in choices and those choices drive behavior.

All of those questions will get people to start thinking about their attitudes. Remember that attitudes always manifest themselves in choices and those choices drive behavior.

PERFORMANCE

Choices and attitudes/mindsets are all well and good, but let's face it—you are in the results business. Results are the direct outcome of the choices we make and the attitudes we have. The road to getting your direct reports to take responsibility ends with a full and complete examination of the results that are created. The purest kind of responsibility-based conversation includes clear expectations followed by excuseless discussion of results. The courageous elements of your leadership will manifest themselves most fully in the questions that you ask regarding performance. Your questions are critical to building a high-performance culture. To help direct your followers to accepting responsibility for their performance, you could ask: What did you do or not do that led to these results? If you could turn back the clock, what would you do more or less of? Of the things over which you had control, which do you think contributed to this success/failure?

> The courageous elements of your leadership will manifest themselves most fully in the questions that you ask regarding performance.

In our work with leadership teams, we often encourage the use of accountability partners to ask each other these sorts of questions. These partnerships are between two people who agree to get together twice a month to talk about their goals and their progress. The idea started years ago when my brother Corey and I got together for dinner and began talking about our frustration with the lack of progress we were experiencing in our jobs. We started getting together for dinner once a week and simply asking each other questions about the goals we had set the previous week. The meetings were not designed to make us feel bad or to catch each other failing, but rather to get us to adopt mindsets of execution and performance. The first few weeks, we saw some minor progress. Over time, our questioning skills sharpened and, with each passing week, the questions we asked were tougher. Consequently, our accomplishments became bigger and quicker-paced.

There is absolutely no way your followers can accomplish what they need to accomplish and learn to accept responsibility if you don't develop the habit of asking big, clear, direct questions delivered in an I-want-you-to-win tone. Your team deserves a leader who is courageous enough to ask and ask often. Like Corey and me, you will get better at this as you practice it, and you will see the results improve over time.

> Your team deserves a leader who is courageous enough to ask and ask often.

Here are five ideas to help you get started:

1. Remember to look at all of your choices and all of their possible consequences. Encourage your followers to do the same.

2. Take a few minutes to think about the attitudes/mindsets that you want to see manifested in your area of influence. Make certain that your expectations for your followers' attitudes are clear and concise.

3. Evaluate the extent to which you ask good questions on a scale of 0 to 10. Practice using questions to challenge your followers to accept responsibility for their performances.

4. Consider finding an accountability partner or having your followers pair up into accountability teams.

5. Talk about choices, attitudes/mindsets, and performance all the time, everywhere.

For a download of a worksheet for this chapter and others please go to www.leadershipisntforcowards.com or scan the QR code.

Leadership Isn't for
Cowards Workbook

CHAPTER **19**

Are You Truly Free?

It might be useful to finish the section on taking responsibility with the idea of freedom. Freedom means choices. It is hard to feel free when there are obstacles in the way. One of the tasks you are charged with is removing obstacles from the paths of those you lead. Too often, your followers' road to results is so full of roadblocks that they find themselves easily discouraged. They find it hard to take responsibility for their choices, mindsets, and results because there really are things getting in the way of their achievement. Your job as their leader is to identify, evaluate, and cope with the obstacles.

For purposes of this book, let's call those obstacles *pinch points*. Think back to when you were a little kid—let's say seven or eight years old. If your parents were like my parents, they would kick you out the front door after your homework was finished and tell you not to come in until the street

> **A pinch point is anything that stops or impedes the desired results.**

lights came on or until you were summoned for dinner, whichever came first. When this happened to me, my buddies and I would inevitably get thirsty during a football game or tree climbing or kick the can. Being unwilling to waste a valuable minute of play, we would rush to the hose in the front yard to get a drink of water. If there were multiple kids waiting for a drink, then sometimes we would kink the hose so the water shut off and the person drinking had to let the next person go. That kink in the hose is an example of a pinch point. A pinch point is anything that stops or impedes the desired results.

Using the hose analogy, let me ask you a question: If you wanted a drink of water and the hose was still kinked, what would you do? I know what you're thinking right now: "Is this a trick question, Mike?

I would unkink the hose!" *Exactly!* You wouldn't run up to the faucet and turn up the pressure, would you? Of course not! All the pressure in the world wouldn't do a bit of good until that pinch point was released.

Organizations are just like that hose. There is a desired flow of productivity you want to get out of your people. There is a specific amount of output you want, and when that is not achieved you leap into action (well, hopefully). Usually, leaders turn up the pressure in the hose. They push their employees harder or offer new programs, initiatives, and incentives to try to push them into compliance. Perhaps you would achieve greater success if you found the pinch points and released them, freeing the flow of productivity. Do your customer service policies really reflect that the customer is most important? Is the amount of paperwork and reports your salespeople fill out really necessary or is it just a habit that has been in place for years? Is there a meeting that happens regularly that is a waste of time or could at least be combined with another meeting? Does your current incentive plan really reward what you want it to reward?

Not only do organizations have pinch points, but individuals do as well. While they are different in organizations than in individuals, they are similarly destructive. The more you push against an individual's pinch point, the more resistance you encounter. In the hose example, as the faucet is turned to a higher and higher level, the pressure increases and the hose begins to fail. Weak spots in the hose begin to leak because all the water has to go somewhere. Pinch points in your organization and followers will create similar backups that, if left unchecked, will eventually explode.

How observant are you of pinch points? How much of your time do you use to diligently examine where the pinch points are in the organization and in your people? Most importantly, how often do you examine your own pinch points? Do you have a belief that limits you? Do you avoid conflict? Do you tend to grow impatient when people aren't as quick as you to catch on or do things? Do you see the negative instead of the positive contributions people make? As another example, many leaders are inefficient because one of their pinch points is a more-is-better mindset. They think, "The more agents we recruit, products we offer, dishes we serve, levels of service we provide, the better we will ultimately do." Then they get overwhelmed and confused and things get backed up.

Your organization will get similarly plugged unless you release the pinch points. What's that you say? Your organization doesn't really have any pinch points? Yes you do; trust me. If you really believe you don't have any, then perhaps that mindset is the first pinch point that needs to be dealt with. Seriously, *all* people and organizations have them. All. Everybody. You, your company, your boss, your boss's boss, your employees, the guy who does your taxes, all people and organizations. (Am I being clear enough?)

So how free are you to examine them? Pinch points can be as simple as too much paperwork or a minor inefficiency on a production line. A pinch point could be a process, a policy or procedure, a person, a tradition, even a way of thinking. Consider a pinch point as anything that slows, impedes, or stops desirable results.

Think now of your own area of influence. Think about what the pinch points may be. Ask your followers. No wait, don't just ask—require them to bring up pinch points. Get them to share with you anything in their area of work that slows things down or makes serving customers, making money, building products, working with other departments, and so on, harder.

I was sitting in a leadership team meeting of a hospitality company, when the general manager made an interesting statement: "I am not suggesting that you talk openly about pinch points. I am requiring it. You will not be seen as a complainer or a blamer as long as you are honest and accompany the pinch point with a suggestion for improvement." Well said! It is critical that you free your people to openly and clearly identify pinch points, but don't let this turn into a blame game; require that they come with clear and well-thought-out solutions. It is their responsibility to not only identify a pinch point but also to suggest a plan to release it. It is your responsibility to be looking constantly at your organization and asking yourself if this or that problem can be eliminated or modified. Remember that a pinch point is anything that slows or stops the desired flow of productivity. It can be a process, person, policy, or program.

> It is critical that you free your people to openly and clearly identify pinch points.

"But Mike," you ask, "what if the pinch point is just a necessary evil?" First of all, I would like to challenge the premise of that question. Most people and organizations see pinch points as necessary evils because they are so used to them that they can't imagine a world without them. When a whole industry maintains a pinch point, it becomes an even greater problem. For years, it was believed that people would not pay a lot of money to mail things. Then FedEx came along and proved that people would pay to get something faster. The mailing industry pinch point was resistance to a new way of pricing things. The television industry's pinch point was a belief that there wasn't any room for more than the three major networks. For years, there were no new shows produced and no expansion in the television industry. The music business once believed that it would collapse if legal digital downloads replaced CDs. All of these pinch points have since been released, and all of those industries have adapted.

First assume that all pinch points can be modified or completely released. Starting with that premise will open you and your team to the greatest level of creativity. Second, ask, "If we were going to release it or modify it, what would we have to do?" Finally, evaluate impact and effort. How much effort will it take to release the pinch point? How much impact will that release have? Which is greater? If it will have huge impact with minimal effort, do it now! Do not hesitate! If it's high-impact, high-effort, put it on track for a long-term objective, but don't use that as an excuse to put it off forever. If it's important enough to address, it's important enough to handle within six months. If there are a lot of low-impact, low-effort pinch points, then knock as many of them out as possible because it will help you build momentum. If it's low-impact, high-effort, work to create a plan for making the pinch point less painful for those affected, especially your customers and clients.

Finally, let's talk about personal pinch points. All of us have them. It is important to identify them and free ourselves from them. What are your areas of behavior that slow your desired results in life, relationships, physical health, work, and so on? Maybe your communication skills are a pinch point. Maybe it's the way you deal with conflict. Perhaps you are an overreactor, an underreactor, or a person who procrastinates. You probably know precisely what they are. If you don't, find someone close to you and ask them. I am very sure that they know. Then return to the suggestions I made about eliminating organizational pinch points and apply them to yourself.

> **You and your organization will be truly free when pinch points are clearly identified and released.**

You and your organization will be truly free when pinch points are clearly identified and released. Here are five ways to get started:

1. Create a culture of expectation that everyone will work to identify pinch points.

2. Expect people to share pinch points along with suggested solutions.

3. Evaluate the solutions using impact and effort.

4. Identify your own personal pinch points. Ask your direct reports to do the same.

5. Create pinch point solutions that improve people's lives on a personal level.

For a download of a worksheet for this chapter and others please go to www.leadershipisntforcowards.com or scan the QR code.

Leadership Isn't for
Cowards Workbook

SECTION 5

ACKNOWLEDGE PROGRESS

In this section, we will explore how important it is to pay attention to the progress your followers are making. We will look at how much more effective you can be when expectations are clear, and we will explore the balance between holding back recognition and over-recognizing. *Acknowledging progress*, the second A in ATTACK, is typically one of those leader behaviors that people understand in theory, but often find difficult to enact. You will find it easier after this section.

CHAPTER 20

How Goal-Driven Are You?

The concept of goals is amazingly simple. I am certain you've heard someone give a speech about goal setting at some point in your career. Maybe you've given those speeches yourself. Yet, how many people still don't have clearly articulated goals written down?

Before you decide this chapter is too basic, read on. This section is less about having goals and more about how you can administer those goals in a way that drives results, starting with how you reinforce the progress and success of your direct reports. Acknowledging progress combines all that we have talked about in Section 3 ("Take Action") and Section 4 ("Take Responsibility") with the ability to connect personally with your people. Acknowledging progress is much more than a pizza, a special parking place, or a bonus. It's about being able to articulate how your followers' progress matters to *you*. There is power in that kind of vulnerability, but in order to see, measure, and acknowledge progress, you have to know what your goals are.

> Acknowledging progress is much more than a pizza, a special parking place, or a bonus.

I must admit that for a while in my career, I thought goal setting and the execution of those goals was part of Leadership 101. I tended to scoff a bit when people asked me to talk about the importance of goals. I thought everyone agreed that goals were basic elements. I thought that everyone had them and knew how to acknowledge progress. I was wrong. My mindset about goals was not shared by as many leaders as I expected. An astonishing number of them did not have deep, clearly articulated, meaningful goals.

Your goals should not only drive your professional accomplishments but also deepen you as a person and as a leader. You need goals that are more personal and have real meaning to you. While a goal to increase brand awareness is important and necessary, it may not be a goal that you are passionate about. So, while we will speak about goals in this chapter, I will challenge you to see them from a different perspective.

Very quickly, let's go over Goals 101: Have them. Make them specific, measurable, achievable, relevant, and timed. Don't have a lot of goals—maybe three or four. Bite-sized is better than super-sized. Most importantly, write them down! Carry them with you on a 3×5 card at all times. Make your direct reports do the same thing. There. That was easy. Now let's move on to the new stuff.

Do not underestimate the power of simple, concise goal setting, and especially don't underestimate the power of writing them down. There is some kind of magic to the writing part. As obvious as it sounds, it takes courage to write down your goals where you will be constantly reminded of them and forced to measure how you are doing. There is also something courageous about holding your people accountable for their goals. That accountability will help you acknowledge progress, both yours and theirs.

Good goals are written down and follow the specific, measurable, achievable, relevant, and timed mantra.

Great goals follow the same five-step outline but are more personal. It's one thing to say, "My department's sales for the first quarter will be X." It takes a whole new level of vulnerability and courage to set a personal goal about yourself, such as, "I will become a more interested and inquisitive listener by the end of the first quarter." That goal is about you as a leader. You can measure it because it will require an increase in the number of questions you ask and because people can tell you if you are making progress. When you look at yourself and your leadership and have goals that are personal to you, your courage will deepen. While progress on external goals gets

> When you look at yourself and your leadership and have goals that are personal to you, your courage will deepen.

you paid and extends your employment, progress on more personal, internal goals makes you a better leader.

Everyone has had a results-driven, goal-oriented leader for a boss. Not everyone has had a results-driven, goal-oriented leader who also has significant self-awareness and sets goals designed to enhance that awareness. You can expect personal development from your followers and encourage them to set goals to make that happen, but you lack credibility when you don't expect the same thing from yourself. It takes courage to openly and clearly look at yourself and to set goals that will impact not only your results, but also your leadership. Goals that move you toward being an outstanding leader are transformational, and the progress you make will affect your workplace as well as every other area of your life.

What is the biggest, most mind-blowing goal you have ever accomplished for yourself? What is the most courageous change you have made in your leadership or your life? This cannot be a job change, a move, or an external achievement. It must be a deeper and more personal accomplishment—one that you can feel. Only you know what that goal was or is. Maybe the biggest change was that you decided this whole "treating people right" thing was necessary and you changed the way you treated people. Maybe you were too nice and you lacked the boundaries necessary to build an excuse-free team, and you decided to change that. Maybe you were the leader who had to control every last detail in the world and you set a goal to be less controlling—to let go of your need to be on top of everything.

> If you can't think of a transformational goal you have set or a change you have made to your leadership, now is the time.

Sadly, maybe you haven't ever been bold enough to go way out on the transformational limb. If you can't think of a transformational goal you have set or a change you have made to your leadership, now is the time. It's the courageous thing to do, and most importantly, your followers deserve it. Most organizations, in my experience, are pretty good at establishing goals that drive the business directly. Some organizations are good at encouraging employees to establish their own goals for personal development. The best organizations ask leaders to carefully answer three critical questions: 1) Who were you as a leader a year ago? 2) Who are you as a leader today? 3) Finally, who is the leader you need to be a year from now? Take the time to set a goal based on these questions.

So how do you make your goals concrete enough to influence behavior? No matter what position or role you have in your life, there are only three ways to do that. Whether you are hoping to influence your own behavior or that of one of your followers, you must work to:

1. Create a new behavior.

2. Eliminate an undesirable behavior.

3. Change an existing behavior.

Clear, actionable goals will always relate to at least one of those three things. It is important that you always determine your desired result and then work with those you influence to align everyone's behaviors with it. It must be clear to everyone involved what the desired result is. Once you have done that, it is not particularly difficult to identify the behaviors to be created, eliminated, or changed if you are insightful in the least. The best way is to be inquisitive. Ask yourself good, solid diagnostic questions: What am I observing in this follower that needs to be stopped? What behaviors are missing from their performance? What are they doing that doesn't need to be stopped but needs to be changed?

Behavior-related goals make it easy to observe progress. The next chapters will deal with how to acknowledge that progress in a way that encourages your followers to keep meeting their goals.

Here are four suggested steps to help you and your followers set goals:

1. Be perfectly clear about your desired results.

2. Determine the behaviors that need to be created, eliminated, or changed to achieve those results.

3. Set specific, measurable, achievable, relevant, and timed goals to enact those behaviors. Encourage your followers to do the same.

4. Train and teach your followers to constantly work toward their goals.

For a download of a worksheet for this chapter and others please go to www.leadershipisntforcowards.com or scan the QR code.

Leadership Isn't for
Cowards Workbook

CHAPTER 21

Are You Too Harsh?

This chapter and the next are really about each end of the spectrum. There are leaders that don't acknowledge progress at all, and then there are those that acknowledge everything, everywhere, even when it isn't appropriate. Neither is particularly courageous. Both are extremes that do not solve problems but instead tend to create them.

Before you read much further, it would be helpful to evaluate which end of the continuum you tend to favor. Do you lean toward the end of the line that doesn't acknowledge progress or the end that gushes with effusive recognition? While I'm certain you would like to believe you're right in the middle, I'm pretty sure you're not. Even if you do your best to perform in a balanced way, all of us have a tendency to go one way or the other. So decide which side you think you exhibit the most.

This chapter deals with those who don't acknowledge progress enough. You live in a goal-driven, accomplishment-focused culture. "What Have You Done for Me Lately?" is not just some old Janet Jackson song, but a regular tune sung by leaders every day. The instant a goal is accomplished, another one pops up to take its place. A lack of acknowledgment can destroy future progress.

A sales organization was having trouble motivating its sales team. It seemed that they just couldn't achieve big numbers. Upon investigation, the sales manager realized that every time the sales team neared their current goal, either the pay plan changed or the goal was increased. This passively discouraged effort and was the main cause of their trouble. Why would the team work harder when they knew their target would always be out of reach?

If you tend to be too harsh, then you find yourself withholding recognition until the goal is completely accomplished. You might also have a tendency to acknowledge the accomplishment of the goal but add something that dilutes the recognition, such as, "Can't wait to see what happens next year!" This takes the focus off of your acknowledgment and shifts it toward the next goal instead, and that is very disheartening for your team.

> Appropriate acknowledgment of progress begins with full and complete focus on the success of what is right here, right now.

Appropriate acknowledgment of progress begins with full and complete focus on the success of what is right here, right now. The recognition must be fully and completely about the success in the present. If you find yourself qualifying your recognition or taking a little back right after you've given it, you are too harsh. If you only really celebrate when the goal is completely finished, then you are compromising momentum.

> Momentum is built by stacking similar behaviors closely together in rapid succession.

Momentum is built by stacking similar behaviors closely together in rapid succession. When my nieces and nephew were learning to walk, I would watch them struggle to stand. Then, with lots of encouragement from those around them, they would take a step. Each step was wildly praised, even though it was pretty unstable. The cheers continued *even* when they fell. We weren't cheering the falling down; we were cheering the incremental progress each step represented. Nobody sat quietly whispering, "Shh! Do *not* acknowledge that kid until she is a walker! If you start acknowledging her now, she will never learn to walk!" Instead, we celebrated every tiny bit of progress toward the goal of walking, and our acknowledgment encouraged the babies to keep trying.

How many times does a baby fail while attempting to learn to walk? Dozens? Hundreds? Thousands? I would say, zero. Babies never fail in their attempts to learn to walk, and I'm not speaking psychobabble like, "They don't fail because they keep on *trying*!" Babies don't fail when they are learning to walk because babies don't *interpret* falling down as failure. They think that falling down is a *part* of walking. It's not an obstacle, it's just something that happens during the process. They keep getting up again because they intuitively get that.

Can you imagine if babies had adult brains? What would learning to walk look like? Baby-with-Adult-Brain stands, overanalyzes how well he stood, makes a spreadsheet or three, then takes a couple steps and falls to the floor. Baby-with-Adult-Brain thinks, "Oh maaan! I guess I'm not a walker! I have tried and tried that walking thing, but I just don't think it's for me! I even went to a seminar on walking, but nope, I still can't seem to do it!" A baby with an adult brain and attitude would likely never learn to walk because he would allow the discouragement to make him give up, even though he'd made a bit of progress.

Later in this section we will discuss how effort is not enough by itself, but first, let's clarify something. As your followers begin to move toward a goal, your recognition and acknowledgment of their progress will have an immediate impact on their momentum. Just as our cheering encouraged the babies to walk, your recognition can help your team keep going, despite setbacks.

I have had many leaders say to me that they fear that pouring on the recognition before the job is done will give their followers the wrong impression. Oh, really? And exactly what would the wrong impression be? That they are doing a good job? That you believe in them? That their incremental success is a sign of great things to come? That you are convinced that you have the right person or team on the job based on the results they have accomplished so far? How is any of that the wrong impression? Believe me; you are never going to have a follower come storming into your office, red in the face and shouting, "I have had enough! No more acknowledgment or support! I won't stand for any more of your encouragement! Just stop! I can't take it anymore!" Acknowledging progress as it happens reinforces your followers' desire to accomplish more, faster so that they can receive even more recognition. They aren't going to turn it down, and it isn't going to hurt their productivity in the slightest.

> Acknowledging progress as it happens reinforces your followers' desire to accomplish more, faster.

The most confusing comment I hear from leaders on the harsher side is, "I'm just not the warm, fuzzy, touchy-feely type! I am a nuts-and-bolts, blocking-and-tackling kind of person!" Hmm. I'm not exactly sure what to say to that, except for the tried and true, "Get over it!" It is not touchy-feely to say, "Thank you." It is not warm and

> It is not touchy-feely to say, "Thank you." It is not warm and fuzzy to share your pride in your followers' accomplishments.

fuzzy to share your pride in your followers' accomplishments. It *is* a great way to encourage results. If it feels unnatural, you will get used to it with practice. If it feels awkward, you will find your stride as you discover the impact acknowledging progress can have on your team. Most followers want to please and look for ways to please. You will get more out of them if they know how to please. You have to let them know what makes you happy as a leader, what you consider to be success.

For some leaders, acknowledging progress finds its challenge in the context of the acknowledgment. Group recognition is harder for some leaders, while others struggle with the one-on-one, face-to-face elements of recognition. Both are equally important, but if I was forced to choose one I would err on the side of perfecting one-on-one, face-to-face acknowledgment. All this takes is practice. There is nothing as powerful as a person hearing directly from the boss an acknowledgment of his or her progress and how that progress improves the overall performance of the team. I challenge you to look at your organization and at yourself. What does your organization tend to do best—group or individual recognition? What do *you* tend to do best? Think of examples of times you have recently demonstrated one or the other. Once you have thoroughly evaluated both, work diligently to strengthen the one that you find the most challenging.

> Keep in mind that the tone of your delivery is the key to making your acknowledgment effective.

Because many people find it very difficult, here are some examples of one-on-one recognition. Feel free to use them. If you have a tendency to withhold recognition or avoid it altogether, these phrases may help. Keep in mind that the tone of your delivery is the key to making your acknowledgment effective. Having a sincere and honest tone makes the comments more credible. It is also important that the tone sounds like you. If it sounds like you have been taking voice lessons from the good witch of the north, then it's likely you won't be believed regardless of how sincere you actually are.

- "I want to personally thank you for the efforts you are making on this project. Your work is not going unnoticed. Thank you!"

- "I hoped that you would flourish in this job, and I thought it might take longer since the job is so different than what you are used to. You are learning fast and your results are showing it. I appreciate your hard work and commitment"

- "From the beginning, you knew that this road would be rough, with many opportunities for distraction and detour. You are doing a great job of keeping the group on task and focused. Thank you for being the kind of person who drives excellence!"

Here are five steps for softening your harshness:

1. Be authentic and honest about your tendency to under-recognize.

2. Remember that meaningful acknowledgment of progress increases momentum.

3. Begin to balance one-on-one recognition with group recognition so that you are practicing both regularly.

4. Steal my suggestions for what to say if you get stuck.

5. Be courageous. Even if it feels uncomfortable, just say it. You will get better at it over time.

For a download of a worksheet for this chapter and others please go to www.leadershipisntforcowards.com or scan the QR code.

Leadership Isn't for
Cowards Workbook

CHAPTER 22

Are You an Over-Recognizer?

If you are great at recognition, you loved that last chapter. You might even be standing on your chair saying, "Yes! Absolutely, Mike! I am *great* at this section!" Not so fast! There are leaders (and you may be one) who are so ready to praise and encourage everybody for everything that their acknowledgment loses its effectiveness. This can come in the form of gushing, fake recognition, or failure to recognize the right people for the right reasons.

GUSHING

You know gushers, don't you? Those chronically chipper people that just love to tell other people how wonderful they are and how much they are appreciated? Gushers are often so syrupy that their sincerity is called into question (if not publicly, then certainly privately). The biggest challenge with being an over-recognizer is that credibility is lost in the love fog that so freely rolls over the people being led. As much as people are demotivated by leaders who under-recognize, there is an equal demotivation factor from leaders who recognize so much and with such flair that it isn't really trustworthy or meaningful.

"Hold it, hold it, hold it! Mike, in the previous chapter you said that people will never complain that they are being over-recognized. Now you're saying that I can be an over-recognizer. So which way is it? Because now I'm confused!" Don't fear! I'm going to make a distinction that makes sense.

The distinction has to do with whether recognition is deserved and based on performance. Recognition is useful because of its quality,

> **Recognition is useful because of its quality, not quantity.**

not quantity. If you are a gusher, you have a tendency to create a lot of fanfare in your recognition, even for very minor achievements. If this is done repeatedly, with that much flair, it will become challenging for your followers to know the difference between big stuff and minor progress. Your acknowledgment of progress must also be honest. Don't invent things to recognize; your employees will quickly catch on and your legitimate acknowledgments will lose credibility. Remember the three points of honesty from earlier in the book: your recognition must be factual, useful for the listener, and constructive. If you make your acknowledgments honest and sized to match the accomplishment, you will be much more effective.

FAKE RECOGNITION

The second problem with over-recognition relates to whether or not it is consistent with your behavior. If you publicly recognize people, but privately are harsh and critical, then you lack recognition credibility and your followers will roll their eyes every time you say something nice. They can smell a lack of authenticity a mile away. If your recognition is so sweet and flowery that it doesn't ring true, your sincerity will be questioned. Your followers will likely think of you as an over-recognizer. Is your acknowledgment of progress something that is part of who you are or does it seem like a bolt-on feature that isn't a part of your core? *Real* recognition and acknowledgment come from your core. You can *feel* them! (Yes, I know. Shudder at the thought of the word *feeling* appearing in a business book.) But that's the road to making your acknowledgment effective, heartfelt, and rationally delivered, while still being consistent with your overall personality. If acknowledgment is going to be received in a way that creates the most motivation, then it must be delivered in a way that lands on target. This simply means that it is centered on your listeners, not on you—and the listeners must interpret that. If they think you're giving recognition to make yourself look like a better leader, it won't work. Praise must be delivered in a credible way. Those receiving it must sense that the acknowledgment comes

> **Praise must be delivered in a credible way. Those receiving it must sense that the acknowledgment comes from an authentic place.**

from an authentic place. They need to trust that you really are proud of them and you really do appreciate what they've done. Without that trust, all the acknowledgment in the world will have zero effect. If you honestly don't see any progress worth acknowledging, look deeper. Find some small thing someone has done that you can really get behind. As you learn to look for progress, you'll get better at it and your acknowledgments will remain authentic.

FAILURE TO RECOGNIZE THE RIGHT PEOPLE

A small company CEO had a great vision for a culture that truly celebrated the value of the people working there. He wanted leadership to adopt the vision and carry it through to all employees. The idea was that each employee in the company should feel valued and critical to the success of the company. The employees would feel like their purpose in life could be carried out, at least in part, by working there.

The vision was right on point. As cultural visions go, it was like it was out of a textbook. The CEO was obviously sincere in his appreciation for his employees, and the amount of acknowledgment given was spot-on.

The challenge came when the CEO got too close to the vision and began to take it so personally that he lost track of whom he was acknowledging. While he did a great job making sure the regular employees felt appreciated, he forgot that the leaders charged with carrying out the vision were just as in need of recognition, support, and encouragement. He continuously urged them to make sure their followers felt encouraged without acknowledging their own progress. The incongruity between his talk about the vision and his relentless pressure on those charged with executing it began to take a toll. The front line received all of the acknowledgment while those charged with executing the cultural vision began to feel like Cinderella. There was lots of hard work and talk about the royal ball, but the leaders themselves weren't invited. Without encouragement or acknowledgment of their progress, the leaders began to buckle under the pressure to create the CEO's envisioned culture, eventually creating gaps in the execution of the vision.

Fortunately, the leaders were amazingly loyal and the CEO very coachable, and what could have been a disaster was turned into a success.

The CEO was able to align his acknowledgment with the needs of his followers, from the top managers all the way down to the floor.

This is a good example of acknowledgment being right in quantity but wrong—or in this case—incomplete in quality. There was much public recognition and acknowledgment of the mid- and low-level employees, but the leaders were excluded from praise. Despite lots of focus on getting the vision right, there was little understanding of the impact of the cultural shift on the leaders being charged with the execution. It is impossible to drive a culture of significance and purpose if the very people driving it aren't experiencing acknowledgment of progress. Changing a culture is a monumental task, and those at the top must feel that the vision impacts them deeply and personally if they are to maintain the energy necessary to succeed. You must be consistent in the distribution of your acknowledgment. If you acknowledge only some of the people and leave others out in the cold, you won't be able to create the kind of momentum that drives a high-performance culture.

Three things are necessary for the acknowledgment of progress to drive performance: honesty, trust, and consistency.

Avoid being a gusher; be honest in your acknowledgments. Do your words of acknowledgment have a sincerity that speaks truth, matches listeners' actual accomplishments, and lifts people up? Do your followers believe that your praise really means something? Do you take the time to make your acknowledgment specific and meaningful instead of throwing around platitudes and empty compliments?

Make your acknowledgment trustworthy. Make your acknowledgment trustworthy. Do your followers have reasonable certainty that you have their backs? Can they count on you to stand behind the things you say? Remember that what you say and do—the good stuff and the bad—is amplified greatly when you are in a position of influence. Your honest, trustworthy acknowledgment of progress will only be effective if you really mean it.

Be consistent; don't overlook any Cinderellas in your acknowledgment. Consistency has to do with how much those under your influence understand that everyone's progress is acknowledged by the same standard.

Be honest, trustworthy, and consistent as you recognize your people and you will build incredible momentum and help them achieve great results.

Here are three ways to get started:

1. Match the degree of your praise to the accomplishment itself. Resist the urge to use flowery, syrupy gushing. Make certain that your recognition is honest and balanced by referring to facts.

2. Make certain that the words of acknowledgment you say publicly are manifested in your behaviors privately.

3. Make certain that all parties to the success are recognized incrementally for the progress they are making—no Cinderellas.

For a download of a worksheet for this chapter and others please go to www.leadershipisntforcowards.com or scan the QR code.

Leadership Isn't for
Cowards Workbook

CHAPTER 23

What, When, and How?

Recognition is as much for you as it is for your followers. It's as much about keeping things in perspective, focused on what matters, as it is making your employees feel valued. It's really about the human, artistic side of business, which, for my money, is the most critical part of the whole equation of courage. Being bold in calling out sales numbers, profit margins, and strategic plans takes courage, for sure. Asking your group to really stretch is critical. Driving results through the business is a big part of what a leader does. But there is nothing quite as courageous as truly understanding and caring about the impact of your words and actions on the lives of those you work with. The humility that comes with making certain that your followers are the company heroes makes your success deeper and more profound. It transcends money and other material rewards—not to say that money isn't nice. You can't spend good feelings, and the bank isn't likely to accept satisfaction in lieu of a mortgage payment; however, the personal effects of your leadership and your acknowledgment of progress are long-lasting and impact not only your followers' work but every aspect of their lives. That is why it is important to know what kind of acknowledgment to give, when to give it, and how.

> There is nothing quite as courageous as truly understanding and caring about the impact of your words and actions on the lives of those you work with.

This is not just about feeling good. While I certainly hope your followers feel good as a result of your acknowledgments, I hope even more that it instills a sense of motivation and momentum. It's impractical and unlikely that people will always feel good at work, just like they won't always feel good at home or at play or anywhere else in their life. I love what I do for a living, but sometimes five or six hours on a plane to get in at midnight to speak the next day doesn't feel good; then someone acknowledges my grueling trip and expresses appreciation for the effort I made to be there. At once, I feel a surge of energy. I'm not suddenly happy about travel and enthusiastic about getting on another plane, but it does create a sense of momentum. It's kind of like someone boosting you over a wall. The wall is still yours to climb, but the boost lightens the load, if only for a moment. It might be just what you need to make that next task a success.

Your followers need that leg up—the boost that will get them over the wall and build the momentum and energy they need to accomplish what needs to be done. I have seen entire rooms transformed and energized by a leader's words of recognition. It is easy to underestimate what you say; it's easy to believe that your words are just words. They aren't. I'm not sure that the impact of your words can be overstated. We've gone over the proper kind of acknowledgment; now we'll discuss how to apply it.

> I'm not sure that the impact of your words can be overstated.

Recognition and acknowledgment, whether they are core values or not, can be developed. You can make them important. As a good friend and former client of mine used to say, "You are the boss of them!" You get to set the agenda, drive it, and hold people accountable for it in your area of influence. It doesn't matter whether your company has a recognition culture or not; you can create one in your domain. Do not cower in the face of the challenge. Be courageous enough to make acknowledging progress part of your personal leadership.

I believe that a relentless commitment to a fully integrated culture of acknowledgment will have top-line and bottom-line impact. Like anything else, though, it requires some structure and guidelines. There are things to remember that will help keep your acknowledgment and recognition meaningful. While the concept is pretty straightforward, making it a regular, balanced part of your leadership is not easy. There are people who say it takes a certain number of days to create a habit. I don't believe that. If an action has enough positive effects, it can become a habit immediately. So don't worry about timelines or deadlines. Commit to it, do the work, and reap the benefits.

It requires consistency and relentless accountability to integrate acknowledgment into your culture. This is one of the few situations when I find that a checklist comes in handy. I use this seven-step checklist with clients to determine the extent to which acknowledging progress is really a cultural habit in their organizations. Use it freely and shamelessly if you like it; there is no need to reinvent it.

1. The first step is to make the acknowledgment of progress as close to the actual event as possible. The closer to the event, the more impact the acknowledgment will have. The longer you wait, the less impact. The idea is to reinforce the behavior as quickly as possible. Remember that momentum is built by stacking similar behaviors closely together.

2. Point out as much specific data and information as you can to support your acknowledgment. General praise like, "You're doing a good job," isn't as powerful as, "The way you responded to so-and-so's account problem is likely to retain them as a loyal customer. Thank you!" The more specific you are, the more targeted it will be and the more powerful it will feel to the person.

3. Whenever possible, do it face to face. It takes more work and time, but the return on investment is huge! The next option is a phone call. Not a voicemail, not a text—an actual conversation. (Imagine that! Actually picking up a phone and talking to the person on the other end!) Just one warning—if you leave a message telling them to call you back, give them some relief from the anxiety they will feel about their boss calling them. Something like, "No emergency. Just wanted to thank you," will do. The third best option is a *handwritten* note. I cannot tell you the impact something like that has on people. If you really want to be over the top, call and then follow up with a note. Finally, if all else is impossible, send an email. It's not as good as the other options, but it's better than nothing.

4. Be authentic and sincere. Do not make someone else remind you to do it or, worst of all, do it for you. There are those who actually ask that someone else write their thank-you notes. Hear this: If you are too busy to personally acknowledge

people in your organization, you are too busy. Do not delegate that task. A board meeting or client call should not trump recognizing the people who make those meetings and calls possible. And no, delegating it is not better than nothing. The more the acknowledgment comes from you, the more credible it will be. Don't think your followers will never know; they always know more than you think. Be authentic.

5. *Never* use acknowledgment, or recognition as a way to make bad news better or as a way to deliver criticism (e.g., "You are doing well in your large account sales, but your small account sales really need work."). That's not acknowledgment of progress. That's criticism with some candy coating. This is the one pitfall I see in most leaders—trying to add a spoonful of sugar to help the criticism go down. It's not courageous. It's a coward's way out, so keep them separate, or your acknowledgments will never gain credibility.

    There are times (I'm thinking of performance reviews in particular) when both seem to come at the same time. In that case, give the bad stuff first, but on a day-to-day basis it is bad form and a bad precedent to try to smooth bad news with a dose of acknowledgment in the beginning.

6. This whole section is about acknowledging progress, not just the accomplishment of the goal. Remember the example of babies learning to walk? They learn to walk because they know that it's a process and they are encouraged every step of the way. Your team's accomplishments, both individually and collectively, will be greatly enhanced if you recognize their progress as they go.

7. Never ever use acknowledgment or recognition as compensation for a screw-up on your part. If you make a mistake, say something wrong, or embarrass somebody in public, do *not* attempt to make up for it by gushing on them, buying them a gift, or giving them the day off. If you mess up, apologize, commit to behavior change, and move on. Don't think that being super nice and complimentary can *ever* make up for your mistakes. It's like having a fight with your significant

other and sending them flowers afterwards, thinking that the smell of the flowers can make up for the stink of the fight the night before. People are smart; they know what you are up to. Instead, go back to the section about how to take responsibility and review it.

I believe your heart is in the right place. Sometimes we just forget or get so busy we don't take the time. I also believe that you want your people to succeed. Part of that success begins with offering the gift of acknowledging progress.

That said, you getting this far in this book is a testament to your commitment to your leadership. You deserve to be recognized for that! Well done!

Here are four steps to help you begin acknowledging progress in the right time, place, and way:

1. Think about your own tendencies around recognition. Do you follow the guidelines on the checklist?

2. Think of several people you can give meaningful recognition to in the next 24 hours.

3. What are two accomplishments in your own life that deserve self-recognition? Do something nice for yourself.

4. Find ways outside of work to acknowledge others. It's good practice and it feels good.

For a download of a worksheet for this chapter and others please go to www.leadershipisntforcowards.com or scan the QR code.

Leadership Isn't for
Cowards Workbook

CHAPTER 24

Are You about Effort or Achievement?

No section on acknowledging progress would be complete without a thorough look at excellence. There is no excuse for mediocrity. The world is full of people and organizations that are willing to settle, but courageous leaders are not. While it is nice to see the efforts people make and important to acknowledge progress, there should be no doubt in your

> To allow the people you influence to make valiant attempts to reach their goals, but still fall short is unfair and weak.

organization that achievement is essential. To allow the people you influence to make valiant attempts to reach their goals but still fall short is unfair and weak. A relentless commitment to achievement at the highest level is a bold and courageous move that will make the progress you acknowledge that much more meaningful.

While acknowledgment of progress is certainly an important and vital part of driving performance, it is not all there is to it. People will not achieve just because you encourage and motivate them. Somebody must drive performance. Somebody must plant the flag on the hill and refuse to accept anything but success.

One day, I had just finished a training session for a group of leaders. I was very familiar with this group, as I had worked with them many times. I had a sense of the culture and how it worked. There was little doubt in my mind that all of the leaders in that room were talented and committed. They were held accountable and their performance expectations were clear. They were expected to accomplish their business goals, as well as to continue their personal leadership development. To add another layer of intensity to the puzzle, they were held accountable for scoring at the highest level on employee satisfaction surveys. These were leaders who knew what they were doing.

This particular session was the final training session for the year. At the end, the most senior-level executive delivered one of the clearest messages I have ever heard. She said, "You all have your goals for next year and you have all seen your employee satisfaction numbers. You know your goals there as well. If you are not crystal clear about our expectations for next year, get with your boss today and get clear. Now, let me be very direct: You will accomplish each and every goal without exception, or you will have a difficult conversation with me—not with your direct supervisor, but with me. Make no mistake; the only way we will thrive in the oncoming unstable economy is if every person in this room steps up and makes a commitment to achieving, even exceeding, their goals for next year. We will do everything we can possibly do to support you in your success, but ultimately it's your responsibility. You have your job here because we believe you can do it. Now go do it! Any questions?"

I would love to tell you the room burst into applause, but it did not. In fact, it was very quiet. I will tell you this: There was absolutely no doubt in that room. Excellence and accomplishment were the only options. The executive had effectively burned the bridges, pointed them forward, and told them, "You win or you die." Some people left that meeting thinking it was a little harsh. Others accepted the message and set about their work unaffected, while still others left challenged and excited. It was fascinating to watch as, month after month, some achieved and some did not. Just as promised, difficult conversations were had and celebration was seen. At the end of the next year, the results spoke for themselves. In almost every category, the organization met or exceeded its mark.

An argument could be made that some people in the organization would have achieved the same results without the direct and blunt message of the year before. But one thing is for sure: There was zero, zip, nada lack of clarity about the organization's commitment to excellence. Everybody knew what they were supposed to be doing.

I am neither endorsing nor challenging the style of the message, but I am advocating the clarity. We have become too soft about our expectations. Parents tell their kids to *just do their best*. Bosses worry about upsetting their employees and so they don't set high expectations. I am in full support of a respectful workplace where people enjoy their jobs and look forward to coming to work, but I am also in full support of less whining and more doing, less passing the buck and more personal responsibility, less explaining why you didn't and more showing how you did. It is the responsibility of leadership to lay out expected results in the most effective and humane way possible. Your direct reports deserve clarity and frank, diplomatic communication about expectations.

> **Your direct reports deserve clarity and frank, diplomatic communication about expectations.**

Be very careful, though. If you go charging into your next meeting all fired up about excellence, but you do not have clear and compelling goals and objectives that meet the criteria we talked about in Chapter 20, you might as well launch your ship directly into the rocks because it's going to sink anyway. Excellence is no accident. It doesn't happen because you say it should or because you give fiery speeches. Excellence happens because every person in your organization has absolute clarity about what the expectations are, how they are measured, and the specific part each person is to play in their achievement. Do not assume that they know; know that they know.

> **Excellence is no accident.**

If you are going to plant the flag and tell them to take the hill, then you had certainly better provide the resources to do it. There are only four reasons anyone in your organization will fail at anything: ignorance, refusal, obstacles, or capability.

- If the problem is ignorance, then quickly and efficiently get them the skills and knowledge they need to accomplish the job. Assess the skill or knowledge deficit and resolve it.

- Refusal means that the follower has been given clarity, knows how to do the job, and is capable of doing it, but chooses not to. That's an issue for human resources, and they need to be counseled out.

- Obstacles are things (pinch points) in the way that need to be removed. Remember, a pinch point can be a policy, a process, a person, or anything else that makes it difficult to get things done.

- Capability, in this context, means the person is incapable of doing their job. Training won't help. Removing obstacles won't help. The fact is that they just aren't capable. They want to, but they simply can't. You have to redesign the job, reassign the person, or hire somebody else. Know this: If they aren't capable, that is often a leader problem because a leader put them in that job to begin with. There are also times when the organization moves past the capability of the person in the job. Do all you can to help them find another job at the company, but move them along.

> In all cases, excellence is the mantra, compromise is not an option, and effort is not enough.

In all cases, excellence is the mantra, compromise is not an option, and effort is not enough. When your expectations are high, your goals are clear, and you acknowledge progress along the way, your organization will move swiftly and efficiently toward your vision for its future.

Here are six ways to drive excellence:

1. Make sure you and those who report to you are absolutely clear about your expectations and how they are measured.

2. Evaluate resources and fill any gaps so that your people can meet their targets.

3. Be emphatic and unwavering in your commitment to excellence.

4. Design and enforce regular accountability around the expectations.

5. If people begin to fail, assess the reason for the failure and use the appropriate interventions.

6. Acknowledge progress regularly.

For a download of a worksheet for this chapter and others please go to www.leadershipisntforcowards.com or scan the QR code.

Leadership Isn't for
Cowards Workbook

COMMIT TO NEW HABITS

The C in ATTACK stands for *commit to new habits*. So often, leaders rehash old strategies. While those sometimes still work, great leaders create new habits. Sometimes it can be as simple as eliminating an old one; other times it can take more effort. In this section, we will explore several new habits to which you need to be committed, including accountability, communicating powerfully, and coaching. You will come to understand what is really involved in committing to positive changes in your behavior and what it takes to have significant impact on the behavior of your followers.

CHAPTER 25

Just How Much Accountability Can One Person Stand?

Blah, blah, blah—everyone is talking about accountability! *We need an accountable culture. There isn't enough accountability in the company. You need to hold that person accountable.* We've already touched on accountability in this book, but we haven't yet explored what it really means. Does accountability really produce its promised results, or is it just one of those buzz words that we all discuss but seldom apply? Is it overrated, or is it a new habit to which you need to commit?

It depends on whether you use it as a positive source of help or as a punishment. It depends on whether you ask great questions and give good direction, or put people on the spot. It depends on you and what you do with it. When used properly, accountability is a gift. It's a present you should give every day in every area of your life.

For years, I had a very passionate belief about people who worked for me. I thought, "I hire people who are qualified for their jobs. I give them the resources necessary to do those jobs, and then I get out of the way and let them do their thing." That belief got me and my employees into a lot of trouble. There was ambiguity about what constituted success and failure. My staying out of the way felt like abandonment and made me appear disconnected. Neither feeling was useful to my leadership. Had I been better at engaging, asking, and holding accountable, more could and would have been accomplished by my team.

So what is accountability and what isn't? How exactly do you *do* it?

Accountability is not about hovering over people. My stepson, Maxx, his mother, and I attended his college orientation session. At the end of a very long couple of days (long in hours, long in information—I thought I could just go sign the papers, pay the bill, and *adios*, but apparently they really want you to pay attention), they sent the kids out of the room and had a psychologist speak to the parents. We'd had so many people talk to us over those two days that another speaker was exactly what I didn't want to hear; however, this guy was fascinating. He stood up in front of us and explained the process of separation—how it was a necessary part of the college experience. Of course, the topics of the entire two days were all about the college experience, but for the most part they covered the technical, scientific elements of that experience—registration, rules, and regulations, finances, and so on. This guy talked about the social and psychological experience (the artistic side, if you remember the distinction from earlier in the book). He used a phrase that has since become very popular: helicopter parenting. Helicopter parenting is just what it sounds like: hovering over your kids all the time, calling them excessively, asking too many questions, being too nosy, and on and on.

As I looked around the room, it was clear that the speaker had our full attention. Then he said, "Don't call them all the time. Don't constantly ask them parental questions like, 'Are you eating? Doing your homework? Brushing your teeth?' They are not high school students anymore. You need to hold them accountable for the big things, such as grades and social appropriateness. But if you hover over them, two things will happen: First, they will become very annoyed. Second, they will begin to avoid you. Neither of those are things you want for a freshman in their first semester of college."

That is a perfect parallel to your leadership. Don't be a helicopter leader unless they absolutely need it. If they need hovering for a long time (unless they are a new employee being trained), they probably shouldn't be in that job anymore. Accountability is different from hovering; it is focusing on the big picture by making observations, asking good questions, and encouraging course correction. Your job is to identify the outcomes you expect and then to develop strategy. Your direct reports' jobs are to commit to the results. Accountability, in most cases, is about making sure the results are achieved.

Don't get nervous if you need to step back a bit. You get to set the parameters for how things are done. Just try to avoid specifically outlining each step. It is best if those you influence are given maximum flexibility in how they accomplish their results. It will insure greater productivity, pride in their work, and momentum to keep getting things done. Hovering over them and trying to pay attention to every dotted i and crossed t will drain you of vital energy and make those you influence crazy. Clarity about results and relentless focus on achieving them, while still allowing maximum flexibility on how that is done, is the most effective way to approach accountability.

> Clarity about results and relentless focus on achieving them, while still allowing maximum flexibility on how that is done, is the most effective way to approach accountability.

Don't get nervous either if you need to step up. This whole book has been teaching you to ask good questions, demand personal responsibility, and provide solid leadership, all of which are parts of accountability. Take what you've learned and apply it. This chapter will take you the rest of the way by showing you the when and the how.

Accountability is as much an art as it is a science. It's as much about how you do it as it is about actually doing it. Accountability is answerability; it is about keeping people focused on what matters and performing in alignment with expectations and performance standards. It is not about busting people; it is not about catching people. It is about asking smart questions and understanding the answers so that you can keep the organization on track. The formula is straightforward: What is the expectation? Did you do it? If so, congratulations. If not, what needs to happen for you to do it?

> Accountability is answerability; it is about keeping people focused on what matters and performing in alignment with expectations and performance standards.

Accountability is not limited to work. Let's say we're going to meet for dinner. We agree to meet at six. At four, I send you a text to confirm that we are still on for six. That's accountability. You and your significant other have plans to go on vacation. You ask if he or she has had a chance to make the reservations yet. That's accountability. You ask your kid in college for their grades. That's accountability. You have a one-on-one with your direct report to talk about progress on a project. That's accountability. Courage demands accountability, and accountability requires courage. If you are going to lead courageously, you must create a highly accountable culture. Hold your people accountable. Not just sometimes. Not once in a while. All the time. Commit to making it a habit.

Sometimes accountability is seen as a tool to use with the low performer. That's absolutely right. Use it with the low performer . . . and with the average performer and with the high performer and with the occasional performer and with the consistent performer. Accountability is not punishment, and it should not be seen as punishment. *Not* holding people accountable is punishment—to them, to you, and to the whole team. It is unfair to let those you lead work without accountability because it lets them settle for less. High-performance organizations are highly accountable organizations, every single time.

How would you rate yourself on the skill of accountability? How would your direct reports rate you? How would your boss rate you?

The balance between the art and science of accountability is delicate, and you should pay close attention to where you stand on both ends of the spectrum. As we talked about in Chapter 2, both the artistic and scientific sides of your leadership are critical. For most, the scientific elements are easier to manage, but in the case of accountability, I have observed both to be challenging.

The science of accountability has to do with the nuts and bolts of it. Are your performance expectations clear? Is there a clear mechanism for measuring success? Do your direct reports understand how to win? Do you check to make sure people achieve their targets? Do you adhere to the expectations and measures you have set in place? Do you ask good questions?

Let's talk briefly about accountability questions. I have said it before and I will say it again: Your power as a leader rests largely in the questions that you ask. It's true in choosing your values, it's true in figuring out your circumstances, it's true in taking responsibility, and it's true in accountability. Great questions always start with a mindset of authentic curiosity; you have to want good answers in order to ask good questions. Questions that start with, "Help me understand…" are always useful, as long as, "Help me understand," isn't followed with "why," as in, "Help me understand why we're behind on this project." That's obviously not a real question; you've already formed your opinion. Instead, you could say, "Help me understand where we

> Great questions always start with a mindset of authentic curiosity; you have to want good answers in order to ask good questions.

are on this project." For obvious problems, "I am confused" questions are usually easier for your followers to handle than "why" questions. "I am confused. I thought we had a conversation last week about getting this finished by tomorrow. Now it isn't on schedule. What happened?" In cases when things are going well and you simply want an update, you can use the same kinds of questions because they are open-ended. Ask the right kinds of questions, and you will be able to have helpful, safe conversations with your followers in any circumstance.

The art of accountability has to do with your style. Does your tone reflect a sincere interest in the success of those that you influence? Are you enthusiastic and supportive of their successes and genuinely concerned about their failures and challenges? Do you coach them up? Up to their highest and best performance?

Asking great questions in a sarcastic or caustic tone of voice will create more problems than it will solve. If your tone isn't right, your attempts to create accountability will fail. Do NOT use anger to hold people accountable. If your followers only get asked accountability questions when you are mad, then they will wait until you are mad to take you seriously. On the other hand, if your accountability is overly nice, sugary, and soft, then your credibility will suffer the same challenges. Being interested, genuine, and enthusiastic has to do with changing your mindset. Remember that accountability exists to help your people do their best. Everything you do in this area should make progress toward that goal.

You should first focus on becoming a highly accountable leader. Holding your followers accountable comes second. Your credibility will erode faster than you can imagine if you don't allow your followers to hold you accountable and if you don't hold yourself accountable.

Lead by example, and your organization's culture of positive accountability will begin to take shape.

Here are five ways to get started:

1. Make certain that your performance expectations are clear.

2. Set regular intervals for both formal and informal check-ins and updates.

3. Practice asking good "help me understand" and "I am confused" questions.

4. Don't be a helicopter; remain flexible about how your people accomplish their tasks. Keep your and their focus on the results/outcome.

5. If you didn't already do so, consider finding an accountability partner for yourself and having your direct reports pair up to keep each other accountable. (Refer back to Chapter 18 if you need a refresher on accountability partners.)

For a download of a worksheet for this chapter and others please go to www.leadershipisntforcowards.com or scan the QR code.

Leadership Isn't for
Cowards Workbook

CHAPTER 26

Do You Need to Be Committed?

Yes, you need to be committed. (I can't speak to your mental health, but I can say this with absolute certainty about your leadership health!)

So what? That's obvious, right? Not so fast! It's not just commitment; it's the things you need to be committed to that are important.

Everything in this book is a road map to high performance. These chapters are full of strategies and methods for solving the problems that prevent or limit that performance. In the big picture, you need to be committed to everything we have talked about in this book, but as it relates to this chapter, there are three habits that are particularly important: 1) solving problems independently, 2) communicating powerfully, and 3) playing well with others. Get yourself and your direct reports deeply committed to all three of them. Are you feeling overwhelmed with this book and you want a place to start? Start here. Do you have direct reports that want to develop themselves? Start here.

SOLVING PROBLEMS INDEPENDENTLY

Problems and conflict are a part of life. If you aren't currently dealing with a problem or eighty, you will have some show up very soon. Problems are a necessary part of leadership because they strengthen your team's ability to persevere. Your job is not to eliminate problems; your job is to solve them. The process of solving problems should be a growth-enhancing experience; you can become a better person and a better leader through developing the way you handle problems. By taking responsibility like we discussed earlier and applying the steps here, you should see an immediate improvement in your performance.

Any problem or conflict can be described as, "I want something and something else is in my way." Whether it's part of the company or your life, all problems are more or less the same thing. "I want my team to perform and they aren't." "I want to get somewhere and there is traffic." "I want to close that deal and the decision maker is out until next week." "I want to get tacos and my girlfriend wants hamburgers." Whether they're big problems or small conflicts, they all boil down to the fact that you want something, and something else is blocking you from getting it.

Problems and conflicts are easier to manage if you have a process to follow.

Problems and conflicts are easier to manage if you have a process to follow. That way you don't have to get upset, riled, or angry over something that's really not a big deal.

Choosing your battles is the first step. Do not get involved in issues, conflicts, or problems that you can't influence or control, or where your interests or your department's interests are not directly impacted. While you may have emotions about the issue, and you might even be indignant about it, your energy should not be directed at a problem when investing that energy can't provide a reasonable return on investment.

Ever found yourself in the middle of a heated argument where you had no real interest at stake? I was in a restaurant recently and heard two people talking about a problem that was going on at work. Both admitted that it had nothing to do with them, but both invested enormous emotional energy into it anyway. It sounded exhausting. If you find yourself engaged in a problem that is not yours and you have no ability to influence it or to create a constructive outcome, then bail quickly.

There are three ways to bail out politely: 1) agree to disagree, 2) listen attentively and ask how you can be helpful, or 3) acknowledge the situation, listen empathetically, and move on. These are all easier to do than they sound and take a lot less energy than remaining involved would require. Help your direct reports to do this, too. Do not be dismissive of their feelings, but rather acknowledge their frustration and coach them on coping strategies. Investing energy where there is no return on your investment is a waste of valuable resources.

Once you've chosen your battles, acting on them is the second part. If it is something where your energy can create a positive outcome, then act quickly. Here are four ways to do that:

1. Remember to choose your battles carefully. Do not invest in the first place in problems or conflicts where there is no return on your investment.

2. Determine what you need and what the other person needs in the solution.

3. Solve the problem by evaluating solutions through two filters: "Is it feasible?" and "Is it practical?"

4. Act on the proposed solution.

5. Follow up and evaluate the outcome.

Here is my biggest warning: Do *not* solve all of your followers' problems. Don't even solve most. Remember that the more you are involved in solutions, the more likely it will be that your reports will depend on you. The more they depend on you, the more they will hesitate when solving problems. If they know you will come in and fix the problem for them, they will wait. They will also feel that you don't have confidence in them. That is a dangerous combination.

> Remember that the more you are involved in solutions, the more likely it will be that your reports will depend on you.

COMMUNICATING POWERFULLY

Communicate powerfully! There are only two parts of this for you and your followers to master: 1) communicate clearly and 2) communicate tactfully. Clarity and tact are at the core of powerful communication, and while we've discussed both at various points throughout this book, they deserve their own section here.

Clarity is the extent to which you say things in a way that leaves no doubt about what you are saying. Clarity pushed to an extreme becomes bluntness, which is why tact must be clarity's constant companion. If you are blunt by nature, you are probably thinking, "I don't like to sugarcoat things!" That's what *all* blunt people say. The problem is that you will offend people. While you might not care about that, there are others who do—you know, like your boss. Real communication is about making a point without the people in the room wanting to escape from you as quickly as possible. If you have trouble with this, refer back to Chapter 21 about being too harsh and apply some of those strategies to your everyday communication.

On the other side of the scale, if you are *so* tactful that nobody really gets what you are saying, you are likely perceived as evasive, and your message might not come across clearly. This is just as frustrating to listeners as bluntness. To balance tact and clarity, it is important to:

- Understand your point in advance of communicating.

- Know your audience.

- Deliver the message succinctly and without harshness.

PLAYING WELL WITH OTHERS

> If you can't get along with people and if your direct reports are always ticking people off, then the culture suffers and the results suffer.

Remember in preschool when the teacher would tell you to play nicely with the other children? That rule didn't stop because you grew up. You still need to play well with others, both at home and at work. The leaders who struggle the most do so because they lack skills in independent problem solving, communication, and getting along with others. The leaders that get into the most trouble especially struggle with playing well with others.

If you can't get along with people and if your direct reports are always ticking people off, then the culture suffers and the results suffer. Have you ever had a person work for you who achieves results but is a virus on a personal level? They are the toughest people to lead. If you keep a top producer and don't correct their relationship behaviors, you will set a dangerous precedent that will infect everyone else. People need to be focused on two things: 1) delivering results and 2) building successful relationships. Not just one or the other, but both. The most effective ways to play well with others are:

- Be actively interested in those you lead.
- Model behaviors that are considerate of other people and departments.
- Do not tolerate mistreatment of others by your reports. Confront it more strongly than you confront failure to meet results.

Here are five steps to get you started:

1. Choose one of the three habits to commit to, starting today.
2. List the first specific step you will take to commit to this habit.
3. Find a person who will give you clear and tactful feedback about how you are doing in this area.
4. Go over these three habits with your direct reports and ask them to do the same exercise I am suggesting for you.
5. In 90 days, measure the results of your new behavior. Hold those you influence accountable for improvement as well.

For a download of a worksheet for this chapter and others please go to www.leadershipisntforcowards.com or scan the QR code.

Leadership Isn't for
Cowards Workbook

CHAPTER 27

Just How Different Are You?

Most companies talk about innovation, differentiation, and gaining a competitive edge. At the same time, many fear actively exploring and doing different things because that requires a certain amount of risk, and most people have pretty specific risk tolerance levels deeply ingrained in them. For some, reading about my skydiving adventure in Chapter 14 was scary. For others, it was exciting. But for almost everyone, it was not a normal, everyday type of story. It was out of the ordinary. It was different.

This chapter is about pushing the envelope, challenging conventional wisdom, and refusing to settle for the way things have always been. You no doubt have people in your organization who are averse to change, constantly singing the familiar song, "We've always done it this way." By this point, though, you should realize that being creative and applying that creativity are necessary parts of your leadership. Challenging your people to constantly think differently is a courageous process. If you can solve problems, communicate well, and play well with others, as we discussed in the last chapter, but you can't challenge your people to think and create, then you are in for a frustrating leadership experience (unless of course you're the kind of leader who prefers people to just keep their heads down and not ask questions, but somehow I don't think you would have gotten this far in this book if you were one of those people). "If it ain't broke, don't fix it" is a deadly way to think. You go on and on, not updating and not changing. Pretty soon, days turn into weeks and weeks turn into years. Then—*bam!*— the marketplace changes, takes you by surprise, and you're playing catch up, all because you didn't want to do different things.

Doing different things has to do with understanding the needs of the people you serve—your customers, employees, and community—and then expecting your followers to think of new, imaginative, even crazy, unrealistic ways to significantly improve their experiences. You should always be moving away from the comfortable routine. Comfort is the enemy of doing different things, and complacency makes you stop there. There is no room for comfort if you are going to do different things.

> There is no room for comfort if you are going to do different things.

"But Mike, sometimes people do things differently just for the sake of being different. That's not a good idea, is it?" Yes, it's a good idea. It differentiates you from your competitors, it keeps you thinking, and it ensures you never fall into a complacent pattern. You may have heard people say, "But, change is difficult!" No, change is not difficult. If you won $15 million in the lottery, your life would change. If you won that much money, I seriously doubt you would say, "Oh my gosh, change is so hard!" When change has obvious benefits, it is easy. Even when change is hard, it's often worth the effort. So how do you start to break out of your routines?

Some people drive the same way to work, eat at the same places, order the same items, and go through the same routine every day and never think twice about it. Doing different things starts with . . . well, it starts with doing different things. Take a different route to work. Mix up your morning routine. Go to a different restaurant for lunch. Order a menu item you've never tried. Stop having the same meeting the same way. Even these little steps will help you start to do different things in your life and in your work. It's all about breaking through the ruts in your way of thinking.

One of my first jobs after college was as a branch manager for a company that helped other companies manage their unemployment taxes. Every year, the branches of this company did audits for their clients to show them how much we saved them in taxes. These audits were a nightmare. It was not an automated process; they were done manually. Therefore, everyone dreaded audit time. We would spend hundreds of extra hours on nights and weekends to get everything done on time.

During one staff meeting, I smiled brightly and asked my staff, "Who's looking forward to doing audits this year?" A collective groan rose from the room. I then put a goal before them by asking one simple question: "If we are going to finish the audits on time and on budget, only work until six on any given night, never work late on Friday, never work a weekend, and still get all of our regular work done, what do we have to do?" After the laughter died down and they realized I was serious, I said we had one hour to figure it out. At first there was dead silence. I offered no suggestions, but I reassured them that as long as my terms were met, we could consider any plan.

At the end of that hour, they had come up with a perfect plan to accomplish every expectation. They suggested that we stop our regular work at four and work from four to six exclusively on audits. Once they fine-tuned the plan, they actually believed we could finish the audits early and even add a couple of unexpected benefits to the clients—and that's exactly what we did. I was amazed at the level of energy that simple exercise created. The audits still had to be done, but setting the goal with the desired boundaries and challenging them to come up with a plan lit a fire under them that surprised even me. The key was to create a simple, straightforward target and then to tell them that we had to do something differently. The same task was completed, but much more efficiently, pleasantly and productively because we broke out of the old routine and tried something new.

What dull, lifeless routines are your direct reports subjected to that are only routines because they are routines? Stop them or change them. Do not allow yourself or your people to accept the status quo. The paradoxical nature of courageous leadership draws you to encourage unique and unusual ways of thinking while still providing a stable environment. You want your followers to explore the edge while being latched firmly to the rock your leadership provides. If you provide solid ground by being tolerant of unconventional answers, occasional disruptions, or creative tangents, your people

> If you provide solid ground by being tolerant of unconventional answers, occasional disruptions, or creative tangents, your people will thrive.

will thrive. The idea is to be consistent and structured about your openness to changing the current routine.

You face a major obstacle. Many creative, different ways of thinking have been extinguished in a lot of people's lives. Re-infusing the people you lead with the desire for unconventional, even radical ways of doing different things is not an easy task. Most human beings are creative thinkers, but that kind of behavior has been driven out of them. Your job is to reignite that—to drive first yourself and then your followers to think differently. Most of that work will be done through the questions you ask. When someone tells you they can't, you ask why not. You teach them to think in terms of opportunities, not obstacles. Creativity is not a suggestion for your followers; it's an imperative. Challenge them, commit to developing this new habit, and hold yourself and them accountable to seeing it through.

> Most human beings are creative thinkers, but that kind of behavior has been driven out of them. Your job is to reignite that.

Here are five ways you can encourage creativity in your followers:

1. Listen:

    a. To customers. Do not ever think that you know more than they do. Design ways to regularly listen to them and to what they say on the street.

    b. To your employees. What are they saying about what needs to change? Drive them to produce creative ideas and solutions.

2. Reward risk. Find ways to recognize people in your organization who do different things. Between the lines, send the message that the risk of failure can be worthwhile.

3. Observe competitors and other industries to get great ideas for different ways to do things. Find ways to draw parallels from different industries and apply them.

4. Read periodicals, blogs, and other commentaries by thinkers you respect. Learn to think like them.

5. Hold employees accountable for sharing ideas about different ways to do things and for creative problem solving. Make this a habit in your organization.

For a download of a worksheet for this chapter and others please go to www.leadershipisntforcowards.com or scan the QR code.

Leadership Isn't for
Cowards Workbook

CHAPTER 28

What's That Weight on Your Back?

The big finale of this section, the one thing that will tie the last three chapters together, is committing to the habit of coaching. Coaching provides a venue for accountability, development of habits, and brainstorming ways to do different things. I am still amazed at how many leaders do not have an authentic, structured, accountable coaching culture. After reading this chapter, you will have zero excuse for lacking one. There is no way you can possibly drive performance if you are not spending one on one time with your followers in meaningful, performance-based conversation. If you are going to be effective, you must be an engaging and compelling coach.

The goal of coaching is pretty straight-forward. It's all about moving people from what they currently do to what you and they realize they *can* do. It's about driving them from their current level of performance to a more desirable state of performance. It's about improving what they do and how they do it.

> There is no way you can possibly drive performance if you are not spending one-on-one time with your followers in meaningful, performance-based conversation.

Coaching is not punishment. It's not required because they have been bad children. It is a helpful, appropriate part of self-development. Unfortunately, our culture still sees receiving help as a weakness as opposed to an expected part of improvement. Coaching is a gift—a benefit of employment—and should be treated that way. I don't know if anything has had a bigger impact on my success than having coaches throughout my life. Coaches have helped me adjust my expectations and see things more clearly, asked me tough questions, and smacked me back into reality, just to name a few of their positive effects. In every case, their counsel has improved my life personally and professionally. It didn't always feel comfortable, but it always created better results.

> Coaching is a gift—a benefit of employment—and should be treated that way.

If you are going to commit to the habit of coaching, there are two things you should know. First, you must accept the fact that you cannot control or change another person. Admit it— you have tried to do that before and failed. We all have! As hard as many people try, there is just no way to force change, so it's best to adjust your expectations now. Your job as a coach is not to change people; your job is to illuminate possibilities and suggest things they haven't thought of on their own. Illuminate those shadowy places where they may be blind. Suggest ideas that can help them improve those areas.

Second, you can be the greatest coach in the world, but unless your coachee is coachable, you are wasting your time. Coachees must be committed to changing in order for it to work. Some years back, a company owner hired me to coach him. In the first few months, he was on time to every session and appeared committed to the work. But then he wouldn't call in for a scheduled conversation. He missed appointments. He continued to say he was committed, but his behavior reflected something different. After a couple of months, it was obvious that he wasn't coachable. What puzzled me was that he refused to stop paying. When our director of operations called to inquire, the company owner said that he felt better being able to say he had a coach. Yikes! That didn't last long, and he had nothing really to show

> You and the person you are coaching have to be willing to do the work.

for the time he had put in. Coaching is about results. You and the person you are coaching have to be willing to do the work. Fortunately, you can help people become more coachable, and later in this chapter I will give you the steps to do that.

Now that you have the right mindset, you understand that coaching isn't a punishment and that your people have to be coachable. It's time to get started.

One of the most important parts of coaching is establishing context. Too often, those being coached don't really understand what the process is about. They tend to resist simply because they have zero understanding of why they need coaching. They must understand why they are being coached. Thankfully, that is pretty simple. Tell them what I told you: coaching provides the opportunity to develop and grow faster so that you can accomplish more of what you want and less of what you don't.

Having a defined process is just as important as establishing context. The person you are coaching will feel more comfortable the more they understand how coaching works. For example, you could tell them, "We will spend forty-five minutes together once a month to discuss anything you would like to discuss. The process works best if you come prepared to talk about an issue or an area of your work that you would like to work on. If you can't think of anything for a particular session, we will brainstorm some areas to focus on. Everything we talk about is designed to help you become better and more excellent at what you do every day." Most coaching sessions include a discussion of the desired result, brainstorming strategies to reach that result, and ideas for how to make those strategies happen. You can also add a discussion of progress made regarding the previous session's topic.

Most often, the process is what makes coaching work. When coachees seem uncoachable, make adjustments to the process in order to help nudge them in the right direction: Meet more or less often. Have shorter or longer sessions. Plan topics ahead, or discuss whatever comes up in the moment. These sorts of adjustments will help your people become more coachable. Make your sessions focused on them; allowing them to talk through the areas in which they most want to improve is often coaching enough.

Here are some ways to make your coaching sessions effective:

- Always remain curious. Your ability to come from a place of interest about everything coachees say will yield the most powerful impact. The power is in the relationship; your interest will encourage them to open up.

- Remain neutral. Keep in mind that your words will carry significant weight, so any time you offer an opinion it will land heavier than you think. Choose your words wisely. Coming from a nonjudgmental place will let those you coach feel free to be completely open. Instead of stating your thoughts, use questions to help them explore alternative ways of seeing things. Unless they are about to drive their careers down the unemployment highway, avoid voicing direct judgments about their thoughts and ideas.

- Point out their strengths and help them build on those ideas.

- Be free from bias, but grounded in belief. For example, a bias would be that all six-month employees are too new to be allowed to work independently. This is a bias against six-month employees. It's too general and it's not fair. Strong beliefs, on the other hand, are necessary for you to build a structure for coaching. For example, I believe that everyone should be given the benefit of the doubt. I believe that change is a choice. I believe that emotional intelligence is something that can be developed. Determine your beliefs about coaching, and they will help you strengthen your process and structure.

- Finally, and most importantly, do not own their issues. Those are theirs to carry; you are just there to help them determine the best way of doing so.

A fraternity had an initiation ritual that tested new pledges' endurance. The pledges were each given a concrete block and told that they must carry it for a full 24 hours. At no time could they put it down. If they did, the time would start over. Some carried it like a bucket. Others hauled it around until it felt too heavy, then they switched arms. But one person took beach towels, wrapped the block, and then attached straps to carry it like a backpack. It was the same size concrete block, with the same weight, but not the same burden.

The people you coach all have concrete blocks. Even you have a concrete block. Coaching is a way of helping people learn how to carry their concrete blocks. It helps them learn which blocks are theirs to carry and which should be set aside. Make sure they leave every coaching encounter with their own concrete block. While there may be times when you can help carry it, keep in mind that it is their responsibility. Taking it for them is a huge disservice, as they will never learn to carry it on their own.

Coaching, the last habit to which you need to commit, is a process of asking questions and helping your people explore, grow, and develop. It will have a long-lasting impact and incredible results. Here are five things you can do to get started:

1. Commit to becoming a world-class coach.

2. Establish the structure that works best for you and your team. The easiest structure for a session is to:

   a. Determine the result you want to accomplish.

   b. Ask questions to find possible strategies.

   c. Explore and suggest actions to enact those strategies.

   d. In the next session, discuss progress.

3. If your organization's culture does not stress coaching, begin to talk about it now.

4. Schedule one-on-one coaching sessions with each of your direct reports at intervals that you can maintain.

5. Do not discriminate based on how well your people perform. Everyone gets time with a coach.

For a download of a worksheet for this chapter and others please go to www.leadershipisntforcowards.com or scan the QR code.

Leadership Isn't for
Cowards Workbook

SECTION 7

KINDLE

The K in ATTACK means "kindle." Courageous leaders are about giving new life to their leadership, their followers' performance, and the way everyone feels about their work. This part of leadership is sometimes overlooked because it doesn't have the "charge the mountain" kind of feel to it that some of the other parts of leadership do. However, the subtlety of kindling will have huge results when it's applied appropriately. In the chapters that follow, you will find strategies to release your energy, influence your moods, make sure things work right, pay attention, and build your relationships. All of this will help you to kindle your leadership.

CHAPTER 29

Is It Really Just an e-Reader?

When I first started working with the ATTACK acronym, I got to K and wondered what that section title could be. What started with K? From somewhere in the recesses of my mind, the word "kindle" popped up. "Kindle?" I thought. "Isn't that an e-reader from Amazon? What does that have to do with leadership? Doesn't 'kindle' mean to start a fire?" I mean, just how many ways can I say, "Light a fire under them"? Hmm, maybe courageous leaders start fires under their people. Nah, that's just too obvious, and about as cheesy as an extra large pizza.

If starting a fire was the only definition, it might have messed up this whole section. However, kindling also means creating new life, inspiring or building passion. That is what this section is about—giving new life to your leadership and to those you lead; inspiring your people to accomplish more and do better. You will notice that I didn't say *flame-throwing* new relationships; I said *kindling* new relationships. *Kindling* means you start small and build up. It is more about a spark than it is about a torch.

Giving new life, inspiring, and building passion: therein lies the high octane fuel that drives every concept covered in this book. Even the habit of playing well with others falls flat without inspiration and energy. When productivity and profit are in full bloom, if there is no inspiration, then there are problems.

Sitting in a meeting, I heard an executive phrase this idea beautifully. She said, "We can do any program, training, or process we want, but without something or someone to breathe life into it, it will fall flat." If your followers don't feel kindled, they will struggle to fully integrate anything. Your ability to give new life to your people and programs will sustain your organization in the hardest times. There is no substitute for the power of inspiration.

> Your ability to give new life to your people and programs will sustain your organization in the hardest times.

Think of Nelson Mandela; Martin Luther King, Jr.; Mother Teresa; and other great leaders. Much of what they did was kindle their followers by inspiring those around them to believe bigger and live larger than they currently were. They unleashed the power of their followers' full energy and commitment.

Everyone holds energy in reserve. They are not always aware of it, but they do. People hold it in check because they may need it for something really important. Your ability to move a group to higher levels of achievement will, in large part, be because you can release that energy.

Have you ever had a long day, thought you were too tired to do anything, and then a friend called with tickets to your favorite play or to a concert you had been waiting to see? All of a sudden, the energy showed up for you. Ever read about a physics-defying act of physical strength that a person used to save someone's life? In both examples, that is the energy that we all hold in reserve. It is the energy that, when released and focused on the right things, creates amazing results. When that is released in your followers, you know you have truly led.

There are many strategies for releasing that energy. Rugby is a sport that we here in America don't pay a lot of attention to, but on the world stage, it's a big deal. The All Blacks, the national rugby team for New Zealand, have an 85 percent win statistic, making them the most successful sports team of any kind in the world, ever. Graham Henry, coach of the All Blacks until his retirement after winning the World Cup in 2011, is the most successful coach in history based on his winning percentage. He was being interviewed at a conference where I was speaking. It was very interesting to hear him discuss his leadership. He spoke of how important it is for his players to be psychologically ready to compete and win. To get them to that place, his team has a pre-game ritual that is world famous—except in my world, apparently, since I had never heard of it. It's called haka, a Maori war dance. This version of haka is both war chant and challenge, and it is customarily performed by the All Blacks before a major game. Graham Henry didn't invent haka, but it is part of the team culture and a very effective means of inspiring them to compete.

Henry understood that while he needed talented players, talent was not enough. To assign them to their positions, make them practice, and then go out and play was not sufficient to win at the highest level. He was able to uniquely understand each player and the group as a whole and help them to release the kind of energy required to be champions. The haka ritual is a unique way that the team synergizes energy for an emotionally charged start to their games.

Interestingly, Graham Henry is not one of those intense, in-your-face coaches. You don't have to be a screaming ball of hyperverbal mania to release power in your people. The skill is in clearly understanding your followers and then providing what they need to win not once in a while, but all the time. You can have the most talented employees and followers in the world, but if you are not kindling them in ways that are unique and based on their needs, you will leave valuable energy and intensity on the table.

The job of kindling falls to you and you alone. It takes courage to slow down long enough to think about the individual needs of each member of your team. You must carve out time to consider the talent you have at hand and create strategies to release that talent in the most effective way. Remember the example of the patio chair? This sort of thinking happens there. It won't happen when you are running to meeting after meeting. It won't happen when you rush through conference calls. It won't happen when you put off coaching and one-on-one time with your people. Inspiration takes more than a poster or a pizza party. It takes patience and energy. It requires emotional investment, observation of what works, the elimination of distractions, and personal relationships. We

> You can have the most talented employees and followers in the world, but if you are not kindling them in ways that are unique and based on their needs, you will leave valuable energy and intensity on the table.

will discuss all of these things in the following chapters. For now, here are four steps to help you get started:

1. Schedule time this week to think about your team. That's all—just think. How is each of them unique? What energizes them? What wears them out? Who is the most underleveraged?

2. Find ways to bring out your people's strengths.

3. Look at possibilities in your people and point those out, too.

4. Think of three things you could do this week to begin to release reserve energy in your followers. What are some of your answers to question one that energize a lot of your people? Use them. What are some unnecessary things that wear out a lot of your people? Eliminate them. Even if you can only release reserve energy in some of the team as a start, their new energy will rub off on everyone else.

For a download of a worksheet for this chapter and others please go to www.leadershipisntforcowards.com or scan the QR code.

Leadership Isn't for
Cowards Workbook

CHAPTER 30

How Are You Feeling?

Would you work in the space your people work in every day? Would you be able to achieve what you expect your people to accomplish, given their conditions and circumstances? Walk around your team's work environment—the actual physical space. Go ahead. I will wait.

Welcome back! So what does the energy in the space say? Does it say "Woo-hoo!" or "Blah"? When you attend your next meeting, what does the energy in the room say? Does it say, "We are here to do important work and we are inspired to do it"? Or does it say, "Oh no, not another meeting"?

As the leader, you have the ability to kindle the kind of energy that your people need to succeed. This is done mostly through the energy you yourself exhibit. Managing your level of intensity and your energy is one of the most inspirational things you can do. You are the leader; your mood and your energy level affect everyone else. You know that your people are talking about you behind your back. You know that the reason the room gets quiet when you walk in is because they were telling a story about you. You understand that you are often the subject of dinner conversation. So let me give you a clue—do not underestimate the power of the energy you exude.

> Managing your level of intensity and your energy is one of the most inspirational things you can do.

"Well, Mike, I am just not a very energetic person." You don't have to be energetic in the traditional sense. This is about the quality of your energy, not the quantity. You give off energy all day, every day. Your followers sense it and react to it. They pay attention *all the time*. Not occasionally, but *all the time*. You may think you are their friend, their colleague, but the fact is that you are their leader. If you don't model the kind of energy and drive you want them to have, you will find yourself very frustrated. "But Mike," you say, "I can't control my emotions." Actually, you can, and I am about to show you how.

Years ago, I was sitting in a staff meeting the day before I was to leave for Maui on vacation. I was not leading the meeting. Have you ever been in one of those situations where you are out in la-la land and suddenly you are asked a question, and you have no clue whatsoever what they are talking about? This was one of those times for me. I realized that someone had asked me a question and I didn't even hear it because my mind was already blissfully on a tropical island. Not wanting to be embarrassed, I conjured up my best defensive voice and said, very professionally, "Whaaaat?" Clearly, not my most profound moment.

"Mike," said a group member, "you're doing that forehead thing you do."

Forehead thing? What forehead thing? He went on to explain to me that when I am impatient or slightly annoyed, I tend to rub my forehead back and forth. When the irritation intensifies, I start to rub my eyes in a not-too-subtle way. When I am about to lose it, I rub my whole face. Are you getting a visual? He said, "You were rubbing your forehead and moving toward your eyes, so we decided we'd better ask you what was up."

Wow! I learned at that moment that my physical patterns communicate a message. I call them mood patterns—physical habits that indicate the moods we are in. These mood patterns are extremely powerful and can be controlled to your advantage.

Not long after that, I was in a bank line in Laguna Hills, California. I realized I was rubbing my forehead. What do you know? I was feeling annoyed. I didn't really want to progress to the eye-rubbing stage, so on a whim, I decided to do something to wildly interrupt my pattern of irritability. I threw my hands in the air and said, "WOO-HOO!" loud enough for those around me to hear.

It worked. I was no longer annoyed (now I just felt stupid, but that is different than annoyed). I wasn't frustrated or irritated, and the action had actually given me a boost of energy.

The elderly lady in front of me (let's pretend her name was Ruth), looked like she might have been present at the opening of the first bank in history. She turned to me and exclaimed, "What are you doing? You scared me half to death!" I told her I was sorry and then explained to her that I had tried to radically change my physiology so that I could alter my mood. She told me that I had certainly altered hers (I'm not sure it was for the better). I asked her how she was feeling and whether she would like to do an experiment of her own. By now she knew that I was either a wack job or just really friendly. Either way, she agreed to my impulsively launched experiment!

"How are you feeling today, Ruth?" I asked.

"I'm feeling a little down," she said. "I haven't heard from my kids in a while."

I said, "Tell me what you do when you are happy."

"I just said I was down. I'm not happy."

"I know, Ruth. Stick with me."

After some discussion, we came up with some things Ruth did when she was happy. They were: smile more, maintain better posture, and spend time with people.

"And today," I said to my newfound friend, "you woo-hoo."

She said, "I do not woo-hoo."

"Just give it a shot," I said.

"We'll get kicked out."

"Nahhh," I answered. "I know the manager." I waved to her. She was now watching and rubbing her forehead.

Standing in a bank line in Laguna Hills, I asked Ruth to change her physiology. I said, "Okay, Ruth, smile." She did. I said, "Now stand up straight."

She said, "This is as good as it gets."

I said, "Okay. You're with me, so that's spending time with people. Now, on the count of three, you and I will throw our hands in the air and say *woo-hoo*. One, two, three!"

She actually did it with me. We both laughed and then she said, "You know, maybe my kids are at home wondering why they haven't heard from me." *Eureka!* It worked. As soon as she was able to put herself in the physical state of being happy, she actually felt happier and more optimistic, and she was able to think of a solution to her problem.

While you might reduce this to "Fake it until you make it," it is really much deeper. The moral of the story is that your physiology directly impacts your psychology. No, I am not talking about body language. Body language is what your body says to others. This is about what your body says to you and your emotions. You have patterns that are a direct reflection of your mood. They are strongly associated with feeling a certain way. If you change your physical pattern, you can change your mood and energy, immediately and authentically.

I bet you know the moods of the people closest to you before they ever say a word. I bet you know your boss's mood the instant she walks through the door. The reason you know those things is because you have observed their physiological patterns—the behaviors they demonstrate when they are in a particular mood. If you pay attention to your own patterns, you can quickly begin to manage your own emotional state very effectively.

> Energy in your organization is the most critical part of driving results, and that energy starts with how you manage yours.

Energy in your organization is the most critical part of driving results, and that energy starts with how you manage yours. I am often asked, "Where does all of your energy come from?" I don't drink coffee. I don't take energy supplements. It's all about applying the strategy I used with Ruth all those years ago. I know my personal strategy for having energy. I make sure there is maximum light in the room, I move at a quicker physical pace, I stay around people, and I practice positive anticipation (thinking that something great could happen with each day and each audience). It works every time. The same thing may or may not work for you. That is *my* strategy for energy. Pay attention to your own moods and energy and develop a system that works for you.

> The art of mood and energy management will kindle your followers, help you maintain positive energy in your organization, and demonstrate that you are the kind of leader who can maintain healthy, positive relationships.

The art of mood and energy management will kindle your followers, help you maintain positive energy in your organization, and demonstrate that you are the kind of leader who can maintain healthy, positive relationships—with yourself and others. Examining and acting on your own physiological moods and their effects on others will have significant impact on those you influence, both at home and at work.

Here are six steps to get you started:

1. List two moods you would like to have more often.
2. Have someone who knows you well help you identify four or five observable behaviors or traits that you exhibit when you are in those two moods. Write them down.
3. As foolish as you may feel, do those behaviors when you are not in that mood and would like to be. I assure you, your mood will change if you sustain the behavior long enough.
4. Now identify one mood you want to feel less. Have someone help you identify the behaviors or traits you demonstrate in that mood.
5. The next time you are in that undesirable space, do the *opposite* of the behaviors associated with that mood.
6. Always make sure that your moods are context appropriate. If you just lost a big contract, coming in happy and enthusiastic may be foolish, but coming in raging may be equally foolish. Shoot for something more like optimism about the future. Context-appropriate energy management is critical.

For a download of a worksheet for this chapter and others please go to www.leadershipisntforcowards.com or scan the QR code.

Leadership Isn't for
Cowards Workbook

CHAPTER 31

Did You Seriously Think That Would Work?

Sometimes you enact a strategy to inspire your people and it fails miserably. Sometimes something looks fantastic on paper, but when you put it into practice, it falls apart. Things like this happen because you weren't properly observing your followers and their needs.

Remember the widget makers from earlier in the book? We talked about how making the widget makers happy was a part of their leader's job. However, there is a part of the widget maker example that we did not address because I wanted to save it for a special chapter. This is that chapter.

When the widget factory was built, they began making widgets. When the demand for widgets started to grow, they had to have more widgets, which meant they had to have more widget makers. Soon, there were so many widget makers that they needed something else. What did they need? That's right; they needed widget-maker supervisors. Why did they need widget-maker supervisors? To make sure the widgets got made.

Well, the market for widgets grew and grew. Then there was a need for—you guessed it—widget-maker managers to manage the widget-maker supervisors who were supervising the widget makers. Why did they need widget-maker managers? Right again, to be sure that the widget-maker supervisors were doing their jobs correctly. Because those widget-maker supervisors were just a little too close to the widget makers.

Then they hired widget-maker directors to direct the widget-maker managers. Those widget-maker directors reported to widget-maker vice presidents, who then reported to the Chief Executive Widget Maker. The traditional widget-making organizations that followed this model believed that more management was the key to better production. They thought their widget makers didn't like to work and needed to be overseen. That philosophy became known as Theory X. Ever worked for a boss like that? Over your shoulder all the time, micromanaging your behaviors and projects, even when you knew more about what was going on than they did? Of course you have.

Then in a land far away, probably San Francisco, someone came along and said, "No! Set the widget makers free! Let them achieve their highest potential! You widget-maker managers, supervisors, vice presidents, and chief executives are in the way of their productivity. We must believe in them, and if we believe enough good things about our widget makers, they will sense our beliefs and accomplish way more than we could have ever imagined. They will be motivated and produce more widgets than could possibly be sold in the land." That philosophy became known as Theory Y.

Of course, both of those theories are used in the real world and not just in Widget Land. Here is the challenge: Both are right and both are wrong.

Very few leaders would admit to being Theory X purists. It just doesn't play well at the company holiday party to espouse a belief that people are lazy and that you as a leader have to stomp out the incompetence so rampant with the workers. It doesn't win you Leader of the Year honors to act like a puppeteer pulling the strings of your followers. But if you are really honest, you will admit that you have a touch of that control-oriented, world domination thing going on. The fact is that most leaders have a little bit of Theory X in them. Call it a residual effect left over from some managers you have worked for in the past. No matter what your age, we are all a little bit on the controlling side, some more than others.

A regional vice president who was renowned for Theory X micromanagement and slave-driving promoted a young man into a high-profile position as the manager of one of the most successful branches in the company. The new manager grabbed the bull by the horns and jumped in with both feet. Sales improved in his branch, customer loyalty increased, and the numbers were fantastic. Clearly this young manager was a star. Almost overnight, the vice president noticed the success. This is how he rewarded it: After closing one night, he went into everyone's offices in the branch, including the new manager's. He went through everything on everyone's desks and placed sticky notes with numbers on them on any work on the desk. The numbers indicated the order that the work should be completed: 1, 2, 3. . . . (I know, you think I'm making this up, but it is the absolute truth.) When the vice president was later asked by his boss why he did that, he said, "I didn't have any confidence that they knew how to get the work done without my direction." The best office in the region, blowing the numbers away, didn't know how to get the work done? Now *that's* a Theory X mindset! As you can imagine, this controlling behavior had no benefit whatsoever and severely damaged the new manager's confidence. Clearly, Theory X purism doesn't work on its own. Believing that it does work will take you down a path of destruction.

Of course, there are organizations on the other end of the continuum as well. A manager in a Midwest healthcare company told her employees that she trusted them to do the right thing and that she would be there if they needed her. Her team was not experienced and began to make a large number of mistakes. The manager continued to encourage them, telling her direct reports it was all going to work out—that everyone makes mistakes. Employees would come to her with questions, and she would answer the questions clearly and with great encouragement. Most often, her direct reports would leave her office feeling better but not particularly certain that they (or she, for that matter) knew exactly what they were doing. Eventually that manager was removed from her position because of the high unchecked error rates. In retrospect, the manager realized that encouragement and support means not only saying "atta boy" and "atta girl" but also requires oversight and critique. Her Theory Y way of leading was no less destructive than the previous example of the Theory X vice president.

If you and I were sitting down for lunch, I'm sure you'd have stories you could tell from both ends of the spectrum. In order to effectively kindle your followers, you need to lead in a way that works properly.

Can your direct reports count on you to give them what they need when they need it? Can they count on you to micromanage them on the tasks on which they need help and to get out of their way when they are winning? Your ability to adjust the amount of oversight and direction you give should always be based on how much that oversight is needed by those you lead. If your doctor misdiagnoses you, she is likely to give you the wrong treatment plan, which can have unpleasant, if not tragic, results. No doctor would prescribe the same medication for every ailment; she adjusts her actions to match your needs. If your child's grades are suffering in math but he or she is getting straight A's in English, you wouldn't hire an English tutor. Can you imagine the futility of hiring an English tutor for your child and expecting his or her math grades to get better? Sounds stupid, doesn't it? Like the doctor–patient relationship and the parent–student relationship, the best leader–follower relationship is based on your level of flexibility—your ability to meet your followers where they are.

> **Your ability to adjust the amount of oversight and direction you give should always be based on how much that oversight is needed by those you lead.**

Often, our relationships with our followers are strained and damaged because we keep putting pressure on them in areas where they have absolutely no need for pressure. Equally damaging is our failure to provide them with coaching, guidance, and leadership in the areas where they most need it. They won't trust our leadership if we don't prove that we can give them what they need in the way they need it. They won't trust us if our methods of leadership don't work.

So how do you make sure you're applying the strategies you've learned in a way that works? *Pay attention.* It's really that simple. Pay attention to what has had a positive effect, and in what circumstances. Be very selective in the amount of pressure you apply and the guidance you give; use it only when appropriate. Remember the idea of a spark? The spark is about the delicate application of the right kind of attention. You wouldn't hold a butterfly in your hand the way you would hold a hammer, and you wouldn't hold a hammer the way you would a butterfly. Use the appropriate leader oversight for the result you are trying to achieve. Your leadership style simply doesn't matter; you can and should have multiple leadership styles, one for each set of circumstances.

The right tool for the right job means the right behavior to drive the right results.

> The right tool for the right job means the right behavior to drive the right results.

In the next chapter, we'll talk about learning to pay attention so you notice what your followers need, but for now, here are five steps to get you started:

1. Identify where you tend to fall on the continuum between Theory X and Theory Y.

2. Before you step in to manage someone, ask yourself how effectively they are accomplishing their expected results. Modify your behavior to reflect that.

3. Narrow your focus to the specific areas of your followers' jobs that need direction. Remember the English tutor example and give them only the help they need.

4. Collaborate with your followers to determine their greatest needs.

5. Adjust your leadership based on the results you hear from them and the results you observe. Pay attention to what works and what doesn't.

For a download of a worksheet for this chapter and others please go to www.leadershipisntforcowards.com or scan the QR code.

Leadership Isn't for
Cowards Workbook

CHAPTER 32

Do You Ever Notice?

Ever notice that it's the little things that make the biggest difference? Ever notice how putting a little more time into getting to know someone can help you both do better and accomplish more? Great leaders notice the little things that improve their followers' performance and the little things that make them less productive. But many people don't know how to *notice*. They overlook the little things because they believe it's the big things that make an impact. Besides, it takes effort to notice the little things; it takes getting to know people.

Chapter 31 spoke about addressing performance needs with carefully applied supervision. It discussed noticing behavior and then coaching your followers based on what they most need. Chapter 30 discussed noticing your own mood patterns and then using those patterns to alter how you're feeling. Noticing others and noticing yourself are necessary steps in the process of kindling—inspiring, breathing life into—your followers. Noticing is a critical nuance. The skill of noticing is certainly about seeing, but it carries with it a certain politeness, courtesy, or interest. It implies that you are motivated by caring. You don't just observe what's happening; you care about the effect it's having on your people. You must be courageous to have that kind of personal involvement and attachment to your followers.

> You don't just observe what's happening; you care about the effect it's having on your people.

So how do you make sure you are noticing?

Have you ever been in such a hurry that you didn't notice something new in your house or the new clothes your partner was wearing? And when he or she asked you about it, you said, "Oh, I didn't even notice." Ever had something stuck in your teeth, or not been able find your keys when they were *right there*, or spent time looking for the glasses that were sitting on your face the whole time? Tell me I am not alone here. Tell me there are times when you don't always notice things. We could say that, in those circumstances, you just weren't paying attention. I would argue that you were paying very close attention. It's just that you were paying attention to something else. Maybe that something else wasn't more important to you, but it was certainly more prominent in your mind.

Some years ago, I went to a doctor because I was concerned about my memory. The doctor, who was approaching retirement, said to me, "Son, I could come up with some technical reason for your memory problem, but it's really very simple. You're putting too much stuff into your head and your brain isn't sophisticated enough to eliminate the right things, so it just gets rid of what it thinks is excess. That's why you're forgetting things." Then he said, "Have a good day, and that'll be $200."

I remember spontaneously laughing out loud. There I was, channeling my inner hypochondriac with all the sincerity I could, and he burst my bubble with a simple explanation—that I was focusing on too many things. My attempts to do more and more created enough mental distraction that my brain just started shorting out. I was so busy, I literally couldn't think straight. My brain was working just fine; my supposed memory loss was because the mental doors were left open and everything was being shoved in. It was like everything that came along was jammed into one room—and I was trying to find my keys, which were in there *somewhere*.

With all the things you are faced with every day, I'm guessing you too have left your brain doors open. Because of that, your good intentions for courageous leadership get left in the background while all the demanding clutter sets up shop in your mind. Ever had someone tap you on the shoulder? Ever had someone keep tapping you on the shoulder? Ever had someone discover that it annoys you so they relentlessly tap you on the shoulder? I have. It is very, very annoying. Just thinking about it makes me annoyed. When your brain experiences the demands of unnecessary clutter, it's like a person tapping you on the shoulder. It's distracting and draining. Each piece of clutter says, "Hey, hey, hey, look at me!" In order to start noticing, you have to rid your mind of that mental clutter.

Your leadership will be enhanced when you choose to clean out the unnecessary so you can notice what is important. You will be able to spend time with your followers to kindle them. You will be able to see the places you need to manage them and the places you need to step back. You will be happier, healthier, and a better leader.

Remember the exercise in changing your mood by changing your physiology? (*Woo-hoo!*) Anxiety, worry, anger, and such are all emotions that clutter your mind. This doesn't mean they should be permanently banished, but holding onto them will fill up your brain, not to mention make you stressed and irritable. Use the strategies I outlined in Chapter 31 to eliminate emotional clutter from your brain.

> Your leadership will be enhanced when you choose to clean out the unnecessary so you can notice what is important.

What about conversational clutter—demands put on your time by people who want to talk to you? I was in the restroom in a major U.S. airport. All men know that when you are at a urinal, you stare straight ahead. It was me and one other guy in the restroom, four urinals down. He asked some generic question like, "Is the weather supposed to clear up?"

I said, "It looks pretty good right now." Then I discovered, to my embarrassment, that he was not talking to me. He was talking on his cell phone. At a urinal!

Really? Come on, man! Are you so busy that you can't even give your bladder a few moments of your time? Nobody's so important—or so unimportant—that they deserve to be called to from a urinal. That guy has got some clutter issues.

Moral of the story: If meetings, calls, and emails are destroying your ability to notice, let some of them go.

Activities, commitments, and everyday tasks can also generate clutter. Keep an eye on how busy you are. When it gets to be too much, you need to cut back. Of course, when you get

> If meetings, calls, and emails are destroying your ability to notice, let some of them go.

to be so busy that you aren't noticing the important things, you might not notice how cluttered you are in the first place. So how do you maintain the kind of clarity to know when you have too much going on in your brain?

Remember the patio chair? You go there. You stop and you step back and you think. It doesn't have to be a place at work. It doesn't have to be a chair on a patio. It can be any moment in time when you pause, relax, and focus on your immediate surroundings.

Sturgis, South Dakota, is the home of the largest motorcycle rally in the world. I am a huge Harley fan and, of course, I have one. In the summer of 2011, I was invited to ride with six of my buddies from Texas to Sturgis for the rally. I was on a prep ride through South Carolina, traveling down a two-lane road through the woods, when all of a sudden, I broke into a clearing. For miles in the distance, on both sides of the road I could see beautiful, rolling pastures. It was 6:15 on a Sunday morning; there wasn't another human being in sight. It was just me, the sun coming up over the pastures, morning mist on the ground, and cows.

My first inclination was to continue powering down the road toward home. After all, I had a goal—a destination, a place to be, things to do, people to see—you get the idea. But something in me said, "Mike, stop and pull over."

So I did. I sat there, all alone on a country road, in complete stillness and quiet. I was struck by the sound of silence. There was no buzz of activity in my head. No hurry. No goal. Just the absolute peace and quiet of that moment, with me and the cows. I was completely aware of myself and my surroundings. I noticed everything. I saw many things—the sunrise, the drifting mist, the cows waking up—I felt the coolness of the morning air and the sound of a train off in the distance. All those things that I would have missed had I let my destination be my driving factor. Being fully present and quiet in that moment was one of the most invigorating experiences I can remember.

You need moments like that! Without those moments of peace and clarity, you will keep on rushing until you burn out, never realizing that you could have stopped, adjusted, and continued with less stress and greater success. These moments will be the times when you notice that your new employee needs some help with his first project, or that your veteran sales rep needs you to back off a bit, or that your morning grumpiness is affecting everyone's enthusiasm. These will be the moments that show you how to kindle your followers and inspire them to greater success. These moments will refresh your ability to notice for the rest of your life.

Noticing matters because your people need to feel significant. It matters because acknowledging human beings and their presence or contribution nourishes the soul and energizes the spirit. In an earlier section, we talked about acknowledging progress. Acknowledging progress is what you do after you notice. Recognition is an external act; noticing is what you do internally. You need to notice things in yourself, and you need to notice things about your team. This clarity is a cherished gift, but it can only be received when you provide space for it. Courageous leaders remove mental clutter, leaving space for self-awareness and noticing things like their impact on others, how their style is received by their followers, and whether or not they are effectively inspiring and breathing life into their organization.

> Noticing matters because your people need to feel significant. It matters because acknowledging human beings and their presence or contribution nourishes the soul and energizes the spirit.

Is your mind clutter-free enough to experience clarity about yourself and your leadership? If not, here are four steps you can take to provide that space for yourself:

1. If you haven't already, find something you love. For me, it's riding my Harley on back roads. For you, it might be a place in the mountains, at the beach, or in a nice room in your house. It can be anywhere, but it must be yours.

2. Go there. Surrender any goal, destination, or outcome. If you clutter your mind with worrying about de-cluttering, you're missing the point.

3. Focus on your full sensory awareness. What are the smells, sights, physical sensations, and sounds? Let yourself notice

each of these. Sense it on every level. Do not evaluate, judge or analyze. Just notice.

4.   Enjoy. You will come away from each of these experiences feeling refreshed, de-cluttered, and aware of your surroundings. Try to do this once a week, both to help you become better at noticing and for your own mental health.

―――――――――

For a download of a worksheet for this chapter and others please go to www.leadershipisntforcowards.com or scan the QR code.

Leadership Isn't for
Cowards Workbook

CHAPTER 33

Ever Given Birth?

I haven't. But the rumors say it's not easy. I have heard that in some cases, it's so difficult and painful that moms in labor threaten the fathers and other people in attendance at the joyful occasion with bodily harm! For some, the process is long. For some, the pain is less severe. For some it's easier; for others it's absurdly difficult. Some deliver naturally; others have a C-section. The point is, any way you go about it, it's a long process that ends with bringing new life into the world. Now that's a miracle!

This section has been about kindling and breathing new life into your followers. We have talked about inspiration and the power you bring to your people when you help them release their reserve energy. We discussed being aware of how your emotional energy affects your followers and how you can change your moods by changing your physiology. You were encouraged to be aware of what your followers need and don't need. Finally, you were advised to let yourself notice things by clearing your mind so that you can be fully present and fully aware. These are all steps and strategies for breathing new life into your followers, but make no mistake—kindling is a process. It is full of ups and downs. Moments of elation are followed by moments of "What was I thinking?"

It's not as simple it sounds. It's not even as easy as just following the steps in this section, because there is always one unpredictable element: humans. At a leadership conference, a man walked up to me and asked, "Can you please teach us how to do leadership without people? Because I would have a great business if it weren't for the customers and employees." He assured me he was kidding, but he had a point. We humans are a little perplexing, aren't we? We have all kinds of

quirks and habits and personality traits that make professional relationships challenging. You can do your best to kindle your followers,
but there is no guaranteed formula for success because we are human
and humans can be unpredictable.

As I have said repeatedly throughout this book, leadership is not
supposed to be easy. It's not going to be sunshine, roses, and puppies.
Giving new life to your followers is tough and sometimes unreward-
ing. Bummer. Stop expecting it to be easy. Understand that building
effective relationships and an excellent work environment is hard.

As difficult as it is, though, there is a huge upside. If you take
the chapters in this section seriously, the rewards will be immense.
More can be accomplished through your ability to inspire your followers and breathe new life into them than you can imagine. It's all
about the way you relate to them. I usually wince when people say,
"It's a relationship business," because it sounds cliché. The truth is,
relationships are business. You relate to your employees, your vendors, your boss, your colleagues, and your customers every day. You
are constantly kindling new relationships, and even your old ones can
be renewed if enough effort is applied. Even damaged relationships
can be repaired.

That renewal, that kindling, happens one step at a time. It happens because the people on both sides are willing to work to make the
relationship healthy and profitable. How much energy are you spending on building your relationships? How much of your mental energy
is used thinking through strategies that will not only deepen but also
broaden the scope of relationships in your business?

> **How much energy are you spending on building your relationships?**

There are two relationships in particular
that you need to kindle: 1) relationships with
your customers and 2) relationships with your
employees. Customer relationship building
draws the organization and its employees into
a closer, more personal relationship with the customer. Does your
organization really know the people that it serves, or does it just know
about them? What specific strategies are in place to draw the customer
to you and you to them? More and more organizations are looking for
ways to get customers involved in the product or service development

cycle. Getting customers engaged is a way to do different things and spark a new kind of connection.

Employee relationship building creates a personal bond between you and your followers. Most of this book has been about ways to strengthen those relationships. What specific processes are in place in your organization to drive the connection between leaders and employees? What have you started doing over the course of reading this book to help kindle those relationships?

Making money is secondary to making your customers, vendors, and employees feel good about their decision to work with you and your company. (After all, if you don't have happy employees and satisfied customers, you won't be in business for very long!) Remember, though, giving life to those relationships is a process. It's not an event. Leaders who expect events to create results are destined to chase event after event, trying to trigger something that can only be created by long-term work and investment.

I like events. I am paid to speak at events. But do yourself a favor and attach appropriate expectations to the events you organize. While your employees may love the company picnic and think it's the coolest picnic they have ever attended, if they go back to work with a boss whose core values are intolerance and greed, it doesn't matter how good the hot dogs tasted. They will still be unhappy and unproductive. If they love the birthday celebrations, but they can't save their data because the new software keeps crashing, then you are going to have a hard time building those relationships.

> Leaders who expect events to create results are destined to chase event after event, trying to trigger something that can only be created by long-term work and investment.

If you want to kindle relationships, you must do several things. You must add significant value to the relationship as they (customers, employees, vendors) define value. You must reduce pain. People will do more to avoid pain than any other thing. Identify the pain in the relationship and work diligently to remove or reduce it. (Adding pleasure will not do as much. Really good pizza will not make up for bad lighting or a complex pay plan.) Finally, you must enhance certainty. People want to count on their relationship with your organization.

If you are not dependable, then the connection will be weak. In a romantic relationship, it's hard to feel all warm and fuzzy if you aren't sure that the other person really loves you. Likewise, if your followers don't know which of your personalities they are going to see in the morning, then a relationship will be hard to build. If your customers don't know if you will fulfill their request in the same way each time, the relationship with them will become strained. The cousin of certainty is consistency; the more consistent you are, the more certain your relationships will be. You can apply everything you've learned in this book, but unless you are consistent in your application, you will not see the best results.

> If your followers don't know which of your personalities they are going to see in the morning, then a relationship will be hard to build.

This consistency is how brand loyalty is built. As I mentioned earlier, I am a big Harley fan. I have only been riding motorcycles since 2007, and by biker standards that's not very long, but I still have brand loyalty. Here's why: My Harley adds value to my life. It provides hours of relaxation. It reduces my pain; if I feel stressed or any other unpleasantness, an hour on that bike relieves that tension. Finally, Harley is consistent. My relationship with the dealership is always easy and fun. When I get my *HOG* magazine, the articles are written with me, the biker, in mind. Every time I walk into my garage, I am *certain* my bike will start. Anywhere I travel, the experience of riding the bike is consistent. Harley has figured out an effective way to kindle customer relationships, and that's part of why they're so successful.

Add value, reduce pain, and create certainty. Which of those areas is the weakest in each of your relationships? Which is strongest? While kindling your relationships is not as physically painful as giving birth, it is definitely a long process. You have to learn to release energy, maintain an optimistic attitude, see what is working and what isn't, and notice the indicators for what you need to change. It takes

> Add value, reduce pain, and create certainty.

years of nurturing and development, just like having a kid. In the end, though, the strong loyalty from both customer and employee is more than worth the effort.

Here are four ways to get started:

1. Get a team of people together and evaluate which group (customers, employees, vendors) is in the most urgent need of a stronger connection to you or your brand. Brainstorm processes that will strengthen relationships with that group. Hint: Make sure your employee relationships are tightest first.

2. Design a system for regularly accessing members of that group. Talk to them about their experience. Don't be afraid to ask what is great and what is missing.

3. Do what they tell you. If you can't do it all, then do some of it.

4. Establish measurements for the new processes and adjust as you go.

For a download of a worksheet for this chapter and others please go to www.leadershipisntforcowards.com or scan the QR code.

Leadership Isn't for
Cowards Workbook

SECTION 8

NOW WHAT?

This last section is designed for you to reflect on what you've read and consider what is next. You have digested a lot of information over the past 33 chapters. Now, take the time to think about what you *want* to do with it all, so you can decide what leadership steps you are *willing* to take. Once you know that, you will be well on your way to being a more courageous leader.

CHAPTER 34

Do You Want To?

Here we are at the last section of the book. We have examined many areas of courageous leadership. These ideas are useful only to the extent that you use them in a way that has impact. Even though you're probably excited and revving to go, it's unlikely you will do everything we've discussed here.

It won't be because you don't want to. It will be because of the many tasks placed on you every day. There is just too much demand for your time, and you can't shove more time into a day. Shoving more stuff into the hours you have is an exhausting exercise that leads to frustration.

Energy, on the other hand, is something that, when invested wisely, can yield benefits of significant proportion. It doesn't take a lot of time to invest energy and reap significant rewards if you carefully target that energy. Similar to what we have discussed previously, there are areas of your life that would benefit from a surge of energy. By cutting out the excess and focusing on what is needed, you can choose which leadership strategies to apply in order to have the maximum impact.

So now comes the time for you to evaluate which part of your leadership would benefit the most from a significant investment of energy. There are many chapters in this book, each designed to address a different area of your leadership. You can choose to focus on any of them. You have the opportunity to make small,

> It doesn't take a lot of time to invest energy and reap significant rewards if you carefully target that energy.

incremental changes in any of the areas we have talked about here. The question is, in which area will you see the greatest return on investment? If you were to make changes in that area, what do you imagine the result would be?

The fact is that small changes, if you maintain them, can have huge impact over time. However, we have a tendency to want big changes. We don't want to lose five pounds; we want to lose twenty. We don't want to read a book; we want to read a book every week. We don't want to run to the mailbox and back; we want to run a marathon. Our New Year's resolutions are always grand, sweeping projects we hope to undertake. Are New Year's resolutions futile? Are they doomed to be broken? Let me save you some time and heartache. The answer is yes.

Here's why: If you can wait until the end of the year to make an important promise, it simply isn't terribly important to you. The list of huge promises we make to ourselves and then, in most cases, abandon a week later, is endless. Our good intentions are usually overshadowed by our tendency to lapse into the comfort of the familiar. Comfort and routine are easy. If you have been with me this far, you know that comfort is the enemy. Discomfort is an indicator of an opportunity for huge positive change. Discomfort gets you to do different things. Hopefully, after reading this book, you are feeling some discomfort about the way things have always been in your organization, and you're itching to make some positive changes of your own.

> **Our good intentions are usually overshadowed by our tendency to lapse into the comfort of the familiar.**

So, besides comfort, what else gets in the way of your desire for lasting and significant change? Are you ready for this? Here they are: enthusiasm and hope. Now, before you accuse me of being a downer, let's explore why these are dangerous. (Relax, I am not going to try to extinguish them from your life. I just want you to be careful.)

First of all, enthusiasm is a fleeting emotion. Long after the initial surge of adrenaline is gone, there is work to be done. Enthusiasm is hard to sustain. It is a good thing—sometimes it gets you started or restarted—but it isn't a constant companion. It will not get you finished. Sometimes you just have to do the work, and if you begin a big project, riding on enthusiasm, you'll run out of gas before you're even halfway finished.

Hope is also a dangerous thing if it's not married to hard work. If you hope the contract comes in, hope the year ends strong, hope your relationship gets better, but don't put in any effort to change those things, you remain on the sidelines. Hope sounds good on a greeting card and may sustain you during difficult times, but real results come from doing the work. I hope to buy a house. I hope to find a job that pays three times what I am making now. I hope to get completely out of debt in 12 months. I hope to go back to school. Many people hope for things and think about changes. Few people go out and make them happen. I suggest action, and action now. Decide, do, adjust, evaluate, and become! Decide the result you want, do the work to accomplish it, adjust your course as you go, and become the leader that kind of commitment creates. Don't sit around hoping; get out there and start doing. Just keep your enthusiasm in check; don't try to do everything at once. Pick one thing to start and build from there.

While enthusiasm and hope and wanting to are not enough, neither is trying. People have come to my office with all kinds of wants that they have tried to achieve. A guy walked into my office one day and said he wanted to lose weight. I asked him how much weight. He told me 20 pounds. I asked what he had tried. He groaned, "I have tried everything!"

> **Hope is also a dangerous thing if it's not married to hard work.**

I asked, "Have you tried standing on your head in a bucket of cow's milk while whistling 'America the Beautiful'? No? Then you haven't tried everything." Thankfully he laughed and understood my point. Of course, that isn't a good strategy for weight loss, but the point is this: Never, ever assume you've tried everything. I guarantee you that you haven't. Also, don't assume that because you tried it once, it will never work. Results require work, not trying. Perhaps my question to that guy wasn't the cuddliest way to start a coaching relationship, but I will tell you this: he lost 25 pounds. It wasn't because he wanted to. It wasn't because I'm such a good coach. He lost the 25 pounds because he was willing to park the *try* and do the *work*.

The battle cry of mediocrity is "I have already tried that." It's a cheap way to avoid doing more work. "I have already tried that" is the close cousin of "I want to." It allows far too much opportunity for an exit. It lets you go on wanting without actually doing. Since we were kids, "at least try" has been ringing in our ears. Somewhere along the way it became an acceptable indication of success. "At least I tried. I didn't actually change anything, but I tried."

While I fully support enthusiasm and hope and wanting and trying, ultimately, none of those really gets things done. What gets things done is work. You have achieved your position as leader because you demonstrated talent, results, promise, or something special that prompted them to put you in your job. Growth as a leader is not automatic. Getting things done involves a decision and a commitment.

> **Getting things done involves a decision and a commitment.**

I believe that the hard part is not in the accomplishment but in the deciding. Decide where you are going to start making changes. Decide how you are going to do that. And then start doing it.

If you really want to, let's look at the five steps it's going to take to make it happen:

1. Clarify a single thing that, if you changed it, would make a *huge* difference in your life and leadership. (If you are having trouble, the next chapter has an exercise to help you do this.)

2. Identify all the pain that will result if you don't change it. (I mean *all*.)

3. Identify all the gain or pleasure that will result if you do make that change.

4. Identify the work required to make that change.

5. Ask yourself a simple question: Is it worth the work? If your answer is no, accept the pain, don't complain, and repeat this exercise. If your answer is yes, get busy doing something about it!

For a download of a worksheet for this chapter and others please go to www.leadershipisntforcowards.com or scan the QR code.

Leadership Isn't for
Cowards Workbook

CHAPTER 35

Are You Willing?

This is the big question. This is what determines how you will answer Chapter 34's question, "Is it worth the work?" It's great that you want to. It's great that you have hope and enthusiasm. What I really want to know is, what are you actually willing to do? Your courage is shown in your willingness. When you run out of enthusiasm and hope and wanting, willingness pulls you the rest of the way.

> When you run out of enthusiasm and hope and wanting, willingness pulls you the rest of the way.

It's time for you to consider your entire journey through this book and ask yourself what you are now willing to do to drive yourself and your followers. What bold step are you prepared to take toward developing courageous leadership? Do not allow yourself the luxury of hesitation. Now is the time to make a firm and unwavering commitment to act in an area of high gain. What problem cannot wait? What have you been pretending not to know that you now realize you must change? Where can you take responsibility? Where can you inspire your followers? What are you willing to do to make those things happen? (Remember that fear of negative consequences is the enemy of willingness. If fear is limiting your willingness, go back to the six-question exercise in Chapter 13 to help you work through it.)

> Do not allow yourself the luxury of hesitation.

So how can you decide what to do, and how do you set reasonable goals that you are willing to meet? The following exercise will help.

HIGH-GAIN ACTIVITY

Your high-gain activity is the one activity that, if you did it all the time, would have the most profitable and productive impact on your work. Imagine that I came to your office and I had a way to force you to do only one thing at work for the next five days. You had to do this one thing all day, every day. Of course, you would want this activity to have the highest likelihood of producing the most productivity and profit. You would want this to be something you're willing to work hard on for a long period of time. So what would that activity be? This is easiest to determine if you choose a chapter in the book as your activity. Which chapter's subject, if you spent all of the next five days working on it, would have the greatest impact on your organization? Alternatively, you can choose the chapter subject that you most need to strengthen. (Keep in mind that this should be an activity, not a goal. If your goal is to increase customer service scores, the activity would be something like spending one-on-one time training associates.)

Once you have identified that, answer this: "How much time, as a percentage, are you currently spending in that activity?" Estimate an average over the past few weeks or months. Be really honest about it.

Now that you have identified the amount of time you are actually spending, consider the amount of time you *need* to be spending. This number is the percentage of your time that you need to devote to this activity in order to achieve the results you want. Don't pick a percentage that you *estimate* is reasonable or practical; objectively determine the percentage the activity would require in order to meet or surpass your goals.

Now find the difference between the actual amount of time you spend on that activity and the amount of time you *need* to spend. It is probably a big number. Most of the time, there is at least a 10 percent gap between the needed time and the actual time. This gap is your leadership efficiency gap; it is the gap between what you could do and what you are doing. The gap drains life, energy, and productivity from your leadership every day. So naturally, we want to shrink the gap.

Let's say the amount of time you are spending in your high-gain activity is 5 percent and the amount of time you want to spend is

25 percent. That's a big gap. Your enthusiasm and your wanting tell you to try to close the gap all the way. Let me take a moment here to share something with you: you are *never* going to close it all the way. You will run out of willingness to keep going before you get there. But what *can* happen is a narrowing of the gap. Even a slight narrowing makes a huge difference. If you could increase the time you spend on your high-gain activity from 5 percent to 8 percent, that's over a 50 percent increase in your focus on the activity. That is huge. And it doesn't seem like such a big change, does it? It seems like something you'd be willing to push through, even when it gets difficult to keep going.

So how do you narrow the gap? There are two questions that will help: 1) What would you have to believe in order to increase the time you spend on your high-gain activity? 2) What would you have to be willing to do to increase that time? Adjusting your beliefs and behaviors is the key to narrowing the gap. Use this exercise to find a small change you are willing to make, and then make it.

Are you concerned that increasing your high-gain activity by only a small percentage won't make much difference? Think of it this way: If we got on a boat in Florida and headed for the Bahamas, but we got off course by 3 degrees, we would miss our destination by many, many miles. Small adjustments over time can have a huge impact. Now imagine driving all of your followers to commit to their high-gain activities just a little bit more. Imagine the collective impact of that kind of focus. As you start making changes and seeing the benefits unfold, your willingness to step out courageously will increase and you will start taking bigger steps. For now, though, you just have to be willing to start.

> As you start making changes and seeing the benefits unfold, your willingness to step out courageously will increase and you will start taking bigger steps.

Here are five steps to do that:

1. Look back over the sections of this book. Choose the chapter with the behaviors that would have the greatest impact on your workplace or that you most need to strengthen.

2. Apply the high-gain activity percentage exercise to that area.

3. Commit to making small improvements over time. Decide what you are willing to do and then do it.

4. Have your direct reports do the same exercise.

5. Follow through. Stick with it until you reach your goal.

———————

For a download of a worksheet for this chapter and others please go to www.leadershipisntforcowards.com or scan the QR code.

Leadership Isn't for
Cowards Workbook

CHAPTER 36

Can You Please Just Get On With It?

So, now what? You know what you want to do and you know what you are willing to do, so now it's time to put the book down and get on with it. First, though, congratulations, and thank you for allowing me to accompany you on this exploratory journey through your leadership. Perhaps sometimes you found me encouraging and at other times challenging. At all times, I have tried to be respectful of what you do every day. You are a courageous person, simply because you are a leader. Getting in front of people and asking them to follow you takes a lot of courage, and you already have that. The rest is just about using that courage in new and exciting ways. You have read the book. Now the real journey begins.

> You are a courageous person, simply because you are a leader.

Before you go, let me share the last trait of the courageous leader, one that will help you keep going when the path is steepest and roughest. This trait is persistence. Persistence means pressing forward, especially in the presence of resistance. In fact, when I think of courage, I think of it as Continuing Onward Under Rigorous And Grinding Experiences. Perhaps the most inspiring act leaders can exhibit is pushing through when the wind is in their face—standing boldly, staring down the naysayers, and charging the mountain.

> Perhaps the most inspiring act leaders can exhibit is pushing through when the wind is in their face—standing boldly, staring down the naysayers, and charging the mountain.

While it is certain that you will fall and you will find yourself weary, it is equally certain that you will emerge victorious if you do not hesitate and do not quit. I assure you, the journey will be worth it. Your life and leadership will be enhanced as you serve those you lead.

You will succeed by relentlessly pursuing the things we've talked about here. By understanding that you are messing with people's lives, you will lead with the humility necessary to cultivate respect for your followers, and respect in them for you. By accepting your circumstances as they actually are, you will demonstrate a commitment to reality that infuses your people with certainty and confidence. By taking responsibility, you will model what maturity and honor look like. By taking action, you will inspire urgency and focus. By acknowledging progress, you will create a space of gratitude and eagerness to achieve. By committing to new habits and doing different things, you will demand the kind of forward thinking that will sustain and invigorate those you serve and lead. By kindling your followers, you will find yourself and your team with renewed inspiration and resolve. By understanding the difference between your wants and your will—and by stepping out accordingly—you will demonstrate the courage and wisdom necessary to make real progress in a time when hesitation and defensiveness seem to be the strategy du jour.

The indicators of your success will be found in the performance of your followers. Don't worry about whether or not they are *getting it*. They will get it as you get it, and as you model it and hold them accountable. They will get it as you emphasize responsibility and expect results, both personal and financial. If they still don't get it, it may be time to part company with them.

Often the courageous road is one that is particularly lonely at first. But once you have led the way there, it suddenly doesn't seem as scary to those behind you. While there will be days when you wonder if they are following you because they believe in you or because they're waiting for you to be taken away to the psychiatric hospital, most days will be filled with the certainty, conviction, and power of your well-defined values. As you lead, they will follow, and the results will come.

> Often the courageous road is one that is particularly lonely at first.

For most of my life, I have lived near the beach, and I have heard surfers talk about something called the impact zone. The impact zone is where the waves break most consistently and ferociously. The bigger the waves, the better the surfing, but the more turbulent and dangerous the impact zone becomes. As the surfers paddle out, they are forced to deal with that zone. Seldom can they press through the face of a wave when it is breaking. Usually it is best to dive under it and let the wave break behind them in all of its threatening power. It is hard work. The very waves that will bring them to shore seem to be completely against them at first, but once they get past the impact zone, the surf is easier to manage as they float over the swells. And of course, the payoff is that they get to ride those big waves right back to the safety of the shore.

The process of becoming a truly courageous leader is similar to surfing. Just like the ocean, leadership has impact zones. Sometimes the waves are more turbulent and ferocious than others. It is not always courageous to think that you are bigger and tougher than the turbulence. Courage isn't always about muscling it; sometimes it's about diving under it. Either way, you are persistently pressing onward, through the waves to the gentle swells and the rewards. Remember that just beyond the hardship and the struggle, you will find the opportunities. Be persistent. Be bold.

> **Courage isn't always about muscling it; sometimes it's about diving under it.**

Be courageous!

For a download of a worksheet for this chapter and others please go to www.leadershipisntforcowards.com or scan the QR code.

Leadership Isn't for
Cowards Workbook

INDEX

Uncertainty:
  clarity reducing, 8
  fear caused by, 74

Validation of conflicting view, 55–56
Value adding in kindling, 195–196
Values:
  artistic side and, 8–9
  behavior reflecting, 12–13
  courage and focus on, 11–12, 14
  culture aligned with, 17–18, 21
  expenditures reflecting, 20–21
  identifying, 12
  impact on others', 7, 14
Virus, follower as, 154–155
Vision of future, 67–68
Voice, tone of. *See* Tone, of voice

Waiting mindset, 60, 80
Warning labels, 85–86
Weight and drag, 48–50, 82
"What Have You Done for Me
    Lately?" (song), 121

What now:
  do it, 203
  energy invested in leadership, 201
  high-gain activity, 208–210
  persistence, 211–212
  results require work, 203–205, 207
  small changes, big impact, 6, 202,
    209, 210
Willingness
  to try, 80
  to work, 207, 209
Woo-hoo!, 176–178, 189
Work:
  results require, 203–205, 207
  willingness to do, 207, 209
Work space, energy of, 175
Worry, as emotional clutter, 66, 189,
    191
Writing:
  acknowledgment note, 135
  goals, 115, 116
  message for practice, 154
  values, 12